Mathematics in Process

Mathematics in Process

Ann & Johnny Baker

Heinemann
Portsmouth, NH

HEINEMANN EDUCATIONAL BOOKS, INC.
361 Hanover Street   Portsmouth, NH 03801
Offices and agents throughout the world

Copyright © 1990 by Ann Baker & Johnny Baker

Library of Congress Cataloging-in-Publication Data

Baker, Ann.
    Mathematics in process / Ann and Johnny Baker.
        p.   cm.
    Includes bibliographical references.
    ISBN 0-435-08306-6
    1. Mathematics — Study and teaching (Elementary)   I. Baker,
Johnny. II. Title.
    QA135.5.B24   1990   90-34373
    372.7'044-dc20   CIP

Published simultaneously in the United States
in 1990 by Heinemann
and in Australia by
Eleanor Curtain Publishing
2 Hazeldon Place
South Yarra 3141

Production by Sylvana Scannapiego,
Island Graphics
Designed by Sarn Potter
Cover design by David Constable
Cover photograph by K. Ranald Simmonds
Typeset by Trade Graphics
Printed in Australia by
Impact Printing

CONTENTS

ABOUT THIS BOOK

FROM PROCESS WRITING TO PROCESS MATHS

Process writing has been around for a while now. Educators, teachers, even parents feel comfortable with it and see the obvious benefits of such an approach. At last children:

- choose and enjoy writing;
- have something to write about;
- use writing to clarify their own thinking;
- develop extended pieces of work, drafting and redrafting until the end product works for them;
- convey real messages to real audiences for real purposes;
- overcome problems involving the mechanics of writing, such as punctuation, spelling and grammar;
- brainstorm, classify and try out ideas until they achieve their chosen goals

No, this is not a book about process writing. But there are important parallels between process writing and what we shall call 'process maths'. For example, taking a process maths approach results in similar effects. At last children:

- choose and enjoy mathematics;
- have something to mathematise about;
- use mathematics to clarify their own thinking (and report their findings to others);

1

- develop extended pieces of work, drafting and redrafting until the end product works for them;
- convey real information/data to real audiences for real purposes;
- overcome problems involving the mechanics of mathematics, such as notation and algorithms;
- brainstorm, clarify and try out ideas until they achieve their chosen goals/solutions.

However, if we want to facilitate children's development in, and use of maths, we need to look beyond the processes of writing. Maths is not just the flip side of the writing coin. It is not enough to assume that by encouraging children to write mathematics, or to use the writing processes of drafting, redrafting, refining, publishing and reflecting etc., there will be a development in their mathematical ability that matches the gains that can be achieved with writing by the process approach.

WHAT IS A PROCESS APPROACH?

Very briefly, process writing is an approach to teaching in the language arts that is built on three main platforms:

- children need to experience the process of writing, drafting, revising and editing;
- children need a sense of ownership, writing about their own topics in ways that they develop for themselves;
- children need to write for readers, as writing for an audience brings a purpose and determines style and format.

These three platforms also apply to process maths. In essence, process maths is an approach to teaching that incorporates the following:

- children need to experience the process of doing maths, of becoming involved with a problem or situation, finding and refining their own methods;
- children need a sense of ownership, using their own experiences, generating their own questions and following their own lines of investigation;
- children need to communicate their methods and results to others, relating their findings to their original purpose for using maths.

In each chapter of this book, a fuller description of process maths is developed by classroom anecdotes that clarify the process of doing mathematics, by frameworks that summarise key aspects of the approach, and through suggestions for action in the classroom.

TRENDS IN LANGUAGE ARTS

The 1980s heralded a new era in the philosophy underpinning the language arts. Research into how children learn language and later how they learn to read and write has culminated in some very exciting changes to classroom practice. A close look at classrooms where 'process writing' and 'shared book experiences' are well established provided us with many starting points and questions that could only be explored by actually trying them in maths lessons, and equally exciting results emerged from our explorations.

The success of the changes in the teaching of writing and reading has been so far reaching and enlightening that it has seemed natural to ask, 'What are the implications of applying current language arts trends in the maths classroom?' This book highlights those aspects of the process writing approach that, together with the shared book experience, have direct implications for the maths classroom.

CONFIDENCE WITH PROCESS WRITING

The confidence that teachers themselves have built by introducing process writing to their language arts lessons is vital to the development of a process maths approach. There now seem to be genuine grounds, from the teachers' point of view, to see beyond the expressive potential of a process writing approach and to review critically the basis upon which the so-called basics of education are built.

Spelling is a good case in point. The process writing approach, although not explicitly teaching spelling, encourages the child and teacher to collaborate in developing the child's facility in this basic area. Instead of spelling lists being imposed, they arise naturally out of the child's need to express ideas and communicate these to other readers.

Again it seemed natural to ask, 'How can teachers cash in on their new-found confidence as writing teachers and become confident teachers of maths?' This book addresses this issue by raising questions and offering answers to some fundamental questions about what is involved in taking a process maths approach in the classroom.

MORE THAN A CATCHPHRASE

There have recently been many criticisms of the catchphrase 'process writing'. Jo-Ann Parry and David Hornsby put it very succinctly in *Write On: A Conference Approach To Writing*:

> Writing is a process. We don't need to refer to a 'process approach' to writing: the terminology is redundant. By referring to a process approach there is the possible inference that it is a particular 'method' of teaching writing or that there is a set procedure or series of steps to follow. When children write, they are involved in a process whether teachers recognise it or not.

This applies just as well to mathematics. We use the term process maths, however, in a broad sense, to emphasise that, just as they do in process writing:

- children need drafting and refining stages before they achieve what it is they are striving for;
- children need to be given responsibility for, and ownership of their work;
- children need a purpose for doing maths.

Discussion is vital in mathematics lessons too. This includes discussing amongst themselves to clarify, extend and refine ideas, strategies and methods of presentation. It also includes teacher-initiated discussion, offering skill development, feedback or support. And last but not least, there are occasions in the mathematics lesson where 'publishing' is essential, for example by showing a model, writing a report, or simply sharing results or methods with the rest of the class.

OVERVIEW

The first two sections of this book describe process maths, first from the viewpoint of the child and then in terms of implications for the teacher.

In Part One, the child's experience of process maths is taken as our starting point. By providing examples and descriptions of what happens in the classroom when process maths is adopted, we hope to clarify the teacher's expectation of the approach.

In Part Two, the implications of process maths are explored and frameworks described that enable a systematic approach to be developed by the teacher. The frameworks summarise general purposes for using mathematics and how to create suitable conditions for learning. Suggestions are also made that enable assessment and evaluation to be maintained while encouraging children to adopt a process approach. The message emerges that process maths as a classroom approach is much more concerned with teaching and learning than it is with the product of the maths syllabus.

Part Three takes process maths into the classroom, continuing on from Part One, and examines its implications for curriculum development and the classroom environment. A variety of activities that emphasise process maths are listed. We also suggest how activities can be developed from published starting points and curriculum documents. For example, if your question is: 'This is the activity in my scheme. How should I use it as the basis for my next maths lesson?', then Part Three will provide helpful suggestions.

Overall, our purpose is to show that process maths provides a means of unlocking mathematical creativity in every child. It is a form of creativity that enables all children to find purpose and meaning in what they learn and to gain the confidence they need to communicate effectively through mathematics in everyday life.

ACKNOWLEDGEMENTS

We would like to thank the staff of the many primary schools in Australia who allowed us to work with their children during the preparation of this book. Their feedback and comments were invaluable in helping us to develop much of what follows. We also had the unstinting help of Margaret Goetze who typed much of the manuscript. Finally, we express our deep appreciation to Eleanor Curtain for her encouragement and advice.

PART ONE

THE CHILD'S EXPERIENCE

- ♦ Introduction
- ♦ Children Getting Involved
- ♦ Young Mathematicians at Work
- ♦ Children Communicating
- ♦ Children Learning from Reflecting

INTRODUCTION

'I began today's lesson by reading the book *Alexander, Who Used to Be Rich Last Sunday* with the class. We'd had a few moans earlier in the week about 'never having enough pocket money' and I thought the children would find themselves in sympathy with Alexander's problem. I was right — the whole class wanted to check that Alexander really had spent $1. They went on to relate the story to their own experiences, some children writing their own Alexander stories, others adapting the theme and ending up rich instead. As they worked, the children used their own methods to add and subtract money. Some worked with calculators, some used the plastic money set and some used pencil and paper. As we reflected on the lesson, Jason summed up the class feeling when he said, "I found the calculator O.K. to help, but I'd really like to be able to do it all in my head!" '

This brief report of a lesson where process maths had been adopted suggests some of the features that typify the approach. The initial impetus in this case was provided by a book, which the children found easy to relate to their own experience. During the lesson the children did their own investigations and were given a choice as to method and means of support, some using calculators, others using concrete objects. The children also recorded their work in the form of stories, which were subsequently shared with other children. Time was set aside for the children to reflect on what they had been doing and what they had learned.

The summary of mathematical activity (see page 11) incorporates the features described here, and adds many others. It provides a quick overview of what we consider to be the essential features of the process approach. But where did it come from and why do we think it so important?

The summary has its origins in much of our earlier work on problem solving where a recurring feature was that of gathering and synthesising models of mathematical activity. More recently, however, we were struck by the applicability of the writing process model suggested by R. D. Walshe in *Every Child Can Write!*

Experience Pre- or Problem	Writing	Draft Writing	Revising & Editing	Product & Publication	Readers' Response	Writer's Attitude
decision to write; growth of intention	incubating rehearsing discussing researching	inc. some revising while drafting	recasting polishing rewriting proofreading	appropriate format, despatched to readers	a response that is conveyed to the writer	feelings and reflections on this whole experience
PRE-WRITING		WRITING		POST-WRITING		

The pre-writing, writing and post-writing stages have much of the essence of doing mathematics. It was also interesting to find that Walshe warns against expecting to find that writing proceeds in neat steps from one stage to another. This is also the case with mathematics. For example, in the middle of an activity, children frequently find themselves stuck, and need to spend time having ideas — incubating, questioning, discussing, even brainstorming — to find their way through.

In this part of the book we want to look more closely at each of the aspects of mathematical activity that the following chart summarises. We feel that developing mathematicians need to:

• experiment with ideas;
• invent their own methods and strategies;
• talk and write about their experiences;

and above all,

• experience success that they can learn from.

These are important aspects of maths. Having established the nature of mathematical activity, we will then be in a good position to explore its implications for teaching.

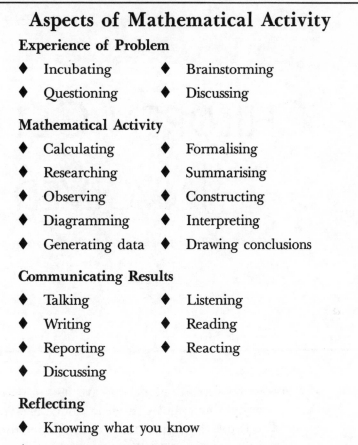

Aspects of Mathematical Activity

Experience of Problem

- Incubating
- Questioning
- Brainstorming
- Discussing

Mathematical Activity

- Calculating
- Researching
- Observing
- Diagramming
- Generating data
- Formalising
- Summarising
- Constructing
- Interpreting
- Drawing conclusions

Communicating Results

- Talking
- Writing
- Reporting
- Discussing
- Listening
- Reading
- Reacting

Reflecting

- Knowing what you know
- Knowing how you know it

1
CHILDREN GETTING INVOLVED

Incubating   Brainstorming   Questioning   Discussing

It is now well accepted in language arts lessons that children have something to write about and can write about it effectively if given time — time to think through what it is they want to communicate, what they need to include and leave out, how to convey their message and to whom they want to convey it.

What happens when we give children the opportunity to take similar initiatives and time to think their way into something that they want to mathematise about? How do children think, talk or work their way into maths?

As we observed children initiating mathematical activity or trying to get involved with a mathematical problem, we found that, rather like Walshe's model for process writing, children incubate, brainstorm, question, or discuss their way into the activity. Their growth of intention and decision to act may be present from the beginning or may develop as they begin to grapple with the activity.

INCUBATING

Just as an egg lies in the incubator with no external signs to give an indication of what is happening beneath the shell, so children may sit apparently disengaged from an activity while in reality there is a great deal going on under the surface.

A TEACHER-POSED ACTIVITY

FREE GROUPING

Give each group some objects to sort in any way that they decide. Encourage the children to talk about what they are doing.

Christopher (age 5) was sitting with a group of children who were sorting a collection of objects. Christopher didn't want to sort. His busy teacher told him he would just have to sit and wait until she could get to him. Christopher sat there sulkily and began playing with some square wooden beads. He took just the red ones, large and small, and began to stack them one on top of another. Soon his tower toppled over. He rebuilt it; it toppled again. Christopher looked more sulky than ever but after some time, obviously spent thinking about the problem, he rebuilt his tower. He sorted his beads now into two groups, large red and small red, and used the large beads for the base of his tower. By the time the teacher got back to Christopher he had sorted all the beads in his own way, using not one but two categories for his grouping, and had a lot to tell his teacher.

What had happened to Christopher was that he had worked and thought his way into a problem that he had posed for himself. This was Christopher's period of incubation.

A PARTIALLY POSED ACTIVITY

A teacher we worked with had started to build up a problem library for her class. Some she copied directly from books, others she adapted to see what would happen if an explicit posing of the problem was omitted, as in this example.

THE SPIDER AND THE FLY

The spider is trying to catch the fly. The spider and the fly move in turn from one junction to another. The spider moves first.

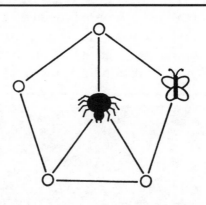

In this case, the textbook continued with,

'Find the fewest number of moves for the spider to catch the fly.'

but this was omitted by our teacher, who wanted to encourage the children to pose their own problems, and not always rely on the book.

The group of 9-year-olds working on the teacher's version began by experimenting with beads, just to see what was going on, and only when they felt confident did they move on to phrasing the problem in their own terms.

David's statement shows that he understood the situation, while Deborah introduced the extra spice of trying to find the least number of moves needed.

Both these examples highlight the importance of making a problem your own and posing your own questions. Initially the problem is 'outside', but after a period of thinking about and dabbling with it a personalised interpretation begins to emerge. The problem is now inside. This can be seen in Deborah's statement.

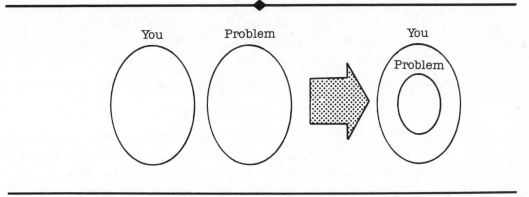

Children experiencing the problem on the outside frequently say,

'What do they want me to do?'

'What are they getting at?'

as if there were some outside authority, a 'them'. In contrast, children who have successfully become involved use language such as,

'I'm going to...'

'I think I'll...'

Spider makes first move
then fly makes his move
Then it's how many moves
it takes to get the fly
                David's Statement

you start with a pentagon with three lines in the pentagon like this ⬠ the spider is in the middle and the fly beside it like on the pentagon above. The idea of the game is the spiders to catch the fly and make as less moves as possible Debrah's Statement.

They have now internalised the problem, and the implication is that they now have ownership of their activity. They want to do something because, in a very real sense, the problem is their own.

A SPONTANEOUS ACTIVITY

Incubation does not just occur at the beginning of an activity. Sometimes the problem may have been posed, but little else seems to be happening. It may need time for the method of tackling the problem to become clear to the child, as happened to Claire.

MAKING SPACE

Claire wanted to make space for a desk in her room.

Claire found a way of working on a problem of her own after a period of incubation. She wanted a desk in her bedroom but her parents had said there wasn't space for one. At school Claire was unusually quiet so the teacher asked her why,

> Claire: 'Oh...I'm thinking about my bedroom. I want my own desk and there isn't any space for one.'

> Teacher: 'Can't you rearrange the furniture in any way?'

Claire shook her head. Later that day she was scribbling little bedroom plans in the margin of her rough book. She was going over and over the problem, drawing, scratching out, redrawing, exploring just one angle of her problem. It was quite obvious to the teacher that Claire was not going to be able to concentrate on her work that day so in the maths lesson Claire was invited to share her problem with the class. The class were interested and decided that they would all like to design their own bedrooms and were given time to think quietly about this. It was during this period that Claire's face brightened. She had just remembered from some time in her past seeing a picture of a bed built up over a wardrobe with a cubby house under it and she began to explore how this could help her. The quiet thinking through and scribbling had opened up another angle on Claire's problem. During this period, she had made various connections with her past experience, her memory of a similar situation, which needed time to filter through to her preoccupation with the problem.

For Claire, this incubation period resulted in a possible solution to her problem, which could now be acted on. She did not think her way into the problem, but out of it.

BRAINSTORMING

Brainstorming — generating ideas by freely associating with a problem or situation — is another way of getting into a problem or activity. The cardinal rule is that brainstorming needs to be non-judgemental. No matter how silly or unrelated an idea may seem, it should be accepted as a potential avenue. After listing all the ideas, the best way of organising them is as a topic web.

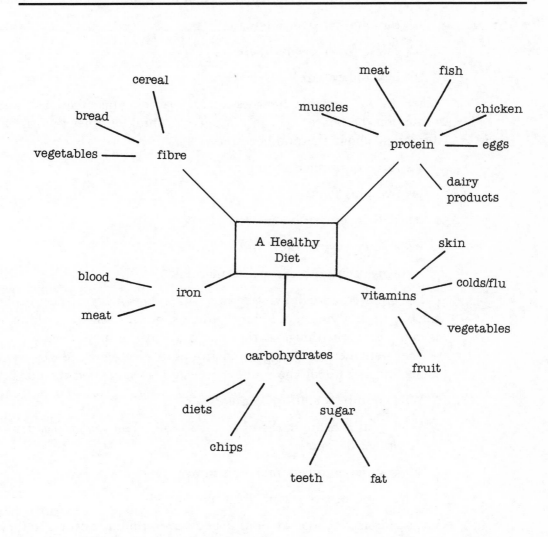

A particular feature of brainstorming is that it encourages a creative and open approach. Too often mathematics is closed and non-inventive or non-creative.

A TEACHER-POSED ACTIVITY

WHAT IS SPECIAL...?
What is special about the number nine?

On one occasion we wrote a large number nine on the board (any number would have done) and asked a class of 9-year-old children what was special about it. The children had no idea what was expected of them so they began to generate what they thought were silly comments,

'It's the number before ten.'

'It's the number of my house.'

'It's how old we are.'

When the children saw that these ideas were being taken seriously and written on the board, they began to try to think of other things that they knew about the number nine,

'It's three multiplied by three.'

'It's five plus four.'

'It's 1001 in binary.'

'It's a square with three rows of three.'

'It's a five-cent and two two-cent coins.'

The children were drawing from a wide range of experiences inside school and, in the case of binary numbers, outside school, to think of as many different things as they could about the number nine.

They were then asked to get into groups to select how and what they could find out about the number nine. Ideas generated included,

'What numbers add up to nine?'

'What numbers are in the nine times table when you go past ten multiplied by nine?'

'What other numbers make a square?'

'What's the binary system Paul mentioned?'

The children were soon anxious to get started finding answers to their questions. They had generated many ideas and a decision to act had been made by most groups.

Brainstorming need not end there — the flow of ideas and questions can continue or re-erupt at any time. For example, the group working on 'What numbers add up to nine' had found about twenty ways, when a voice said,

'We could find ways of taking away to make nine too...a hundred take away ninety-one leaves nine.'

and was echoed by,

'Yeah, and divide and multiply.'

'Add and take away together.'

'We could use a calculator and make hard ones!'

A PARTIALLY POSED ACTIVITY

HEALTHY EATING
How can we be sure we are getting a healthy diet?

A Year 6 class working on diet in a Health Education lesson wanted to know how they could be sure that they got a well-balanced diet, enough fibre, calcium, protein etc. A brainstorming session generated lists of random related words: 'fish', 'vitamins', 'fat', 'fruit', 'dairy products', 'fruit'...The children clustered these into groups on a topic web (see page 17).

Soon it was decided that each group would research and make recommendations about what foods and how much of each are needed for a healthy diet. Again, brainstorming had resulted in the growth of intention and a decision to act.

A SPONTANEOUS ACTIVITY

NUMBER TRAILS
The children use a map of the local area, with a route marked on it, and a list of clues that help them locate environmental numbers/shapes.

A Year 5 class had just come back from their first number trail, prepared by their teacher, and were feeling disappointed. They'd liked the idea and loved being out of school but hadn't felt interested in some of the questions on the number trail, while others were too easy. We encouraged the teacher to let the children brainstorm why they were dissatisfied and what an exciting number trail would be like. It took no time at all, once invited, for the children to brainstorm what was wrong with the number trail. Ideas about what would have improved it were more difficult to generate, and at first were very general, for example,

'Harder questions.'

'Some puzzles or riddles.'

but eventually focused on more specific ideas, such as,

'Instead of asking, "Where can you see the number 240?" questions like "Can you find a number that is in the 10 times and 12 times table. It's less than 250 and more than 200?" would be harder.'

'I would have liked to copy the tessellating patterns I found...or make rubbings or something, not just write where they were.'

'I think the answer to one clue should lead you to the next place like a real treasure hunt. It's too easy when it says "Go to the Estate Agent".'

Soon the children were so excited they developed the intention of making their own 'maths trails'.

QUESTIONING

Sometimes an event, puzzle, story, object etc. can arouse curiosity. Questions such as,

'What's this for?'

'Why did that happen?'

'What if...?'

arise, questions that the children generate themselves and really want to find answers to.

A TEACHER-POSED ACTIVITY

We took a 'baffler' from the local paper into one classroom to see what the children would do with it.

THE HUNGRY MOUSE

This hungry mouse plans to eat every cheese lump, by travelling in six straight lines. If he were smarter, he could start from a different point — and complete the cheese chase in just FOUR lines. How?

When the children had solved this puzzle, we asked them to think about whether they could change it in some way, extend it or make it harder. The following questions were amongst those generated,

'Could we do it with 3/5/7/ lines?'

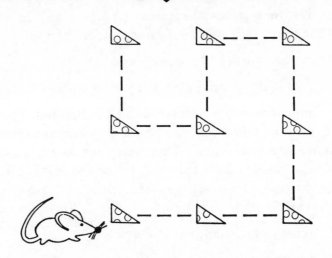

'What would happen if we used more cheese lumps...and made a bigger square?'

'What happens if the cheese lumps are in a rectangle? Would it still take four lines?'

The children were surprised at how easily they had made up new puzzles and wanted to start investigating them. From simple questions the growth of intention and need to act had developed very rapidly.

A SPONTANEOUS ACTIVITY

CLASS BOOK OF RECORDS

After consulting the *Guinness Book of Records*, the children could develop their own Class Book of Records.

A Year 5 class who had been using the *Guinness Book of Records* as the basis for measuring activities found the records fascinating and began to wonder about their own records. Encouraged by us, they decided to think about what class records they would like to investigate. At first many of the questions that they asked were very closely linked to those in the *Guinness Book of Records*, such as,

'Who has the longest hair?'

'Who is the tallest?'

The children were clearly not fascinated by their questions. Suddenly a new slant was provided by one child who said,

'We know who's the tallest in our class. Everyone knows it's Sharon. She's not the fastest runner though.'

They then turned this round and asked,

'Isn't it the people with longest legs who run fastest?'

Immediately the children wanted to find out, but thought that such an investigation would need time for planning and executing, time not immediately available. They were then asked if there were any other similar questions that they would like to investigate. The suggestions made, though not really looking for records, were clearly inspired by the records that they had read about, for example,

'Which hair colour is strongest?'

'Are boys taller than girls?'

'Are boys stronger than girls?'

'Can people run further than they can walk?'

'Can you keep a ball in the air longer by hitting it with your hand or with a bat?'

From the groans when the bell went, it was obvious that the children were ready to get started on finding answers to their questions. Some of the children began to try to answer their questions in the playground.

There is a great deal of potential in encouraging children to pose their own problems. Frequently, what may appear to be a simple dead-end question can, by changing parts of it, lead to some interesting mathematical work. The recent book, *The Art of Problem Posing* by Stephen Brown and Marion Walter, focuses on this topic and, although aimed at university level, suggests a general approach to posing problems that can be usefully employed in the primary classroom. In Part III, we look at this area in more detail; for the moment, we only want to make the point that, for children to become involved in mathematical activity, they need to be encouraged to pose their own questions, either by adapting textbook problems or by bringing their own questions and interests into the classroom.

DISCUSSING

Children always seem to have a lot to talk and argue about. Discussions arise that are never resolved satisfactorily. Quite often though, given the chance, children can investigate the situation being discussed to provide reasoning or evidence to strengthen their argument. Discussions also arise as the result of problems with an activity, for example how to become unstuck, or how to check or compare results.

Research into children using language in this way refers to discussion as 'talking to learn' (see, for example, *Language, the Learner and the School* by Barnes, Britton & Rosen). It is via discussion that children can talk their way into understanding, clarifying their thinking as they talk, share ideas and develop a commitment to action.

A TEACHER-POSED ACTIVITY

FLIPPING TRIANGLES

What pathways can you make by flipping a triangle over its edges?

We suggested this activity to a class of 10-year-olds. The children dived straight in and began randomly flipping triangles that they cut from paper. It soon became clear to them that they weren't getting anywhere.

Tania: 'Look, Claire, what's the point when your triangle is different from mine?'

Claire: 'What are we supposed to be doing anyway?'

Little by little the children in the group talked their way into a line of investigation. Their discussion focused on:

- which triangles to use — an equilateral triangle was chosen;
- the need for a triangular template — the children made their own from stiff card;
- the need for recording — isometric paper was eventually chosen and notches cut in the templates to help keep track of the moves;
- how to share the workload — some to flip and others to record.

By working together and talking about their difficulties they had come to an understanding of what they would aim to do.

A PARTIALLY POSED ACTIVITY

HOW DO YOU MAKE A STAR?

At an appropriate time of year, provide an assortment of materials with which the children can make 2D and 3D decorations.

Working with a class of 7-year-olds who were preparing their room for a Christmas party, we noticed a group discussing how a star should be made. Some children had very rigid ideas about what a star was and what it should look like. The discussion, lively at times, focused on how many points a star should have, where stars are found and what they look like, whether they have to be solid or whether just an outline will do, whether they need to be flat. The only way the group could settle this issue was to do some research and make some stars, and this was the conclusion that they themselves reached. They needed to take action to demonstrate and justify their ideas and points of view.

The children's starting point was the need to make a Christmas star. Each child had a fixed idea about what was required, but it was through discussion that they realised that there were alternative ways of designing a star that needed to be considered. The discussion seemed to help them move from their own egocentric views towards an understanding of what was needed to cater for others. In a sense, they had discussed their way into the problem.

A SPONTANEOUS ACTIVITY

POCKET MONEY
What is a fair amount of pocket money?

As we entered a classroom just before the bell one morning, a cluster of 9-year-old children were having a heated discussion about pocket money. Mark didn't think it was fair that he didn't get as much pocket money as everyone else. We asked the rest of the class later that morning what they thought was a fair amount for pocket money. Initially, outrageous amounts were specified but then the children began being realistic and raised issues about what pocket money was for, what children had to buy with their pocket money, how much parents could afford, what jobs they had to do for it. As the children discussed this topic they became quite sensitive to the issues discussed. Some realised how well off they were, perhaps for the first time; some realised that as they didn't have to buy their own chips and ice-creams etc. they were actually better off than they thought; and some, who received little or no pocket money, began to see some of the reasons for that. Towards the end of this session the children agreed to the suggestion that they should look into the question of pocket money more fully. The children had talked themselves into an understanding of the situation and a need for action.

THE LAST SAY

In the days before the process approach to writing, it was assumed that children had to be given topics to write about. We remember topics from our own school days,

'Water',

'Stranded on a Desert Island',

'A Conversation between a Vacuum Salesman and a Reluctant Customer'.

Another inspiring technique was the starter sentence,

'One day a sixpence fell out of a pocket and rolled down the street...'

It was presumed we had nothing of interest or worth to write about spontaneously. We now know that children can write freely and well about things that interest them, if time is set aside for them to mull over what they want to write about, what they want their writing to achieve, who they want to write to or for. This period of thinking usually results in a growth of intention and a decision to act. That is, the children think, draw and talk their way into knowing what they want to write about and why they want to write about it, as well as how and where to begin.

We hope that in this chapter we have shown that children also have something to mathematise about — if given the chance, time and encouragement. The children can become involved in:

- teacher-posed activities, tailoring them to suit their own levels of mathematical development and their own personal interests;
- partially posed activities, which clearly leave room for the children to negotiate the direction they want the activity to take;
- spontaneous activities, which come directly from the children themselves.

The important point is that whether the activity is teacher suggested or suggested by themselves, the children must take ownership of it. They must want to work on it, want to communicate about it. If theirs is the decision to act, they will want to succeed in finding satisfactory solutions.

◆

2

YOUNG MATHEMATICIANS AT WORK

Calculating/Formalising   Researching/Summarising
Observing/Constructing   Diagramming/Interpreting
Generating data/Drawing conclusions

◆

Despite the look of their polished proofs to theorems, all mathematicians experiment with ideas, pursue blind alleys and make mistakes. Occasionally, very occasionally, mathematicians share their experiences with us (see, for example, 'The Seven Bridges of Konigsberg' by Leonard Euler, in *The World of Mathematics, Volume 1*), but on the whole the process by which they arrive at results or methods of finding a proof, the rough calculations, the data generated to find examples of a theory, the diagrams drawn and discarded, all are hidden. What is presented is the finished, polished result. This near obsession with hiding the process used to pervade maths teaching. Layout and presentation, at least in our day, used to score as highly as correctness — always the prize — and rough work was rubbed out, even discouraged. In the process approach to maths, however, experimentation, pursuing blind alleys and making mistakes are valued equally with the finished result. We want children to attend to what they do, the process by which they reach results or understanding, just as much as they attend to the product of their work.

Under the title for this chapter, we have listed ten types of activity that occur when children do mathematics. The list serves to emphasise that doing mathematics has many facets. In the descriptions that follow, we have grouped the types of process in pairs. This helps to emphasise that in the course of an activity, children will use more than one process, and the combinations that we have chosen do seem to occur quite frequently together. But other pairings or larger combinations are also likely. More importantly, we have used the examples to illustrate various steps that children take towards reaching their solutions. These are the mathematical equivalents of the drafting and editing steps of the process writing approach.

CALCULATING AND FORMALISING

Although the ultimate aim is for children to be able to express the steps and results of calculations in formal notation, we have to encourage them to move towards closer approximations of this notation in their own way. First attempts should be treated as first drafts and be allowed to undergo successive refinements until children are satisfied with the accuracy of what they have written.

TRADITIONAL RHYMES

Many rhymes can be used as starting points for mathematical activity.

As an example of this process of refinement, we were working with a group of 5-year-olds, taking as our starting point the rhyme,

Six little apples
Hanging on a tree
A strong wind blew
And down came three.

and asked the children to write the corresponding formal number sentence,

$$6 - 3 = 3$$

Working with counters the children experimented with different ways of partitioning six. Before long they wanted more freedom.

The children began using larger numbers of apples as their starting point. David chose fifteen as his number and initially had great difficulty counting out fifteen. He spread out a handful of counters and could not keep track of which he had counted and which he had not. He tried setting out and counting his counters in twos and got as far as ten when he lost the counting rhythm. He set out two more counters and went back to the beginning to count again. Now he was under way, 2, 4, 6, 8, 10, 12, two more, 14, and one more, 15. Here David was in effect drafting. His first attempt at counting out didn't work, but he persevered and found an approach that did provide a solution to his problem.

Radha chose to illustrate $9 - 4 = 5$.

'I know about six,' said Radha. 'My brother's six, so it's easy. I want to try with nine apples.'

Although she seemed quick to describe a group of up to three objects, anything over that needed counting. Perhaps this was why, in her first draft, she drew six rather than four apples on the ground. As we shared the rhymes, David pointed at Radha's picture, saying,

'That's funny for four apples.'

Radha did a quick re-count and revised her picture. She didn't think of just crossing out two apples, she crossed them all out and then very painstakingly and carefully counted out four apples. On the other hand, as Hayden was explaining his picture to the rest of the group, he realised that it didn't show what he had intended. He quickly crossed out three apples.

The other children, observing these alterations, checked the groupings on their own pictures. Comments, revisions and redrawing by other members of the group followed and we completed the session by helping each child write their improvised rhyme as a caption for their picture. The resulting pictures and rhymes made a useful book which, for a while, took pride of place in the Maths Interest Centre.

RESEARCHING AND SUMMARISING

The process of researching is important in maths as children often need to collect information before it can be summarised. Research involves generating information by means of measuring, calculating, or comparing; or gathering information from surveys, books and other sources. To summarise the information collected, the children will be involved in classifying and representing their information in a format that makes it clear to themselves and others.

HALLEY'S COMET

Sometimes a topical event can stimulate mathematical activity.

A class of 11-year-old children decided that they wanted to have a class outing to sight Halley's Comet. After very little research, they produced a plan for the outing that their teacher felt would lead to a very disappointing trip. Her approach was to hold a discussion with the children. Rather than just telling them that their plan wouldn't work, and telling them what to do about it, she asked,

'Does it make any difference where you see Halley's Comet from?'

'What do you need for a good sighting of the Comet?'

These questions, and the discussion they generated, were sufficient to set the children thinking again. Nothing had been taken away from the children; it was still their idea, but they realised that their initial draft was weak in a number of ways, and that a redraft was needed. Soon they were asking themselves questions that led to much more tightly focused research,

'Where would be the best place to sight it from?'

'How will we get there?'

'What time would be best?'

'How will we know where to look?'

'What instruments will we need to take with us?'

As the children followed the news of the comet in the media, they began to realise that the 'when' and the 'where' changed as time went by. By now, however, they were sufficiently involved with the problem for their teacher to be able to suggest that draft plans could be shared between groups in pupil-pupil discussions. Further drafts of their plans were developed in this way.

To summarise their information, the children decided to make a chart showing the best viewing times, which days should have the clearest sighting and what time the comet should be clearest. They studied the Southern Cross to identify the key stars so that they would know where to look. Each evening they practised this from media accounts of where the comet was positioned. The children also planned their own transport, accommodation at a campsite and costing. The planning complete, they then wrote a summary of their plan in letters to the Education Department and their parents, to seek permission for the trip. As the children discussed the detailed wording of the letters, one child suggested that the letter would have more influence if supporting charts, tables and costings were included.

As a result of their research, they had discussed and debated amongst themselves the best time and place. They had used charts, maps and calendars to substantiate their proposals. They had written summaries of the information collected, written instructions for using a compass and kept records of the weather and weather trends to try to forecast the best conditions. They had put their case to the Education Department and their parents for permission to turn their plans into action. And action was what they got — the outing was a great success, despite limited sighting of the comet.

Just as important as the product of their research was the process by which the successful outcome had been achieved. The flow diagram below summarises the process that the children went through. It is included to emphasise that in maths, as in writing, the path to an appropriate solution may not be clear at the first attempt. Rather we should expect avenues of research and summaries to be amended as flaws in the argument become apparent. Above all, we should support children as they falter, backtrack and change direction, as these stages are an integral part of mathematical activity.

Beginning	Desire to see Halley's Comet
	Rough plan made
	Teacher's questions
Researching	Children's questions
	Many avenues researched
Summarising	Information sifted
	Extra information collected
	Recommendations formed
	Letters written
ACTION	Halley's Comet sighted

OBSERVING AND CONSTRUCTING

Arthur Owen is always a welcome speaker at maths conferences. As a hobby, he spends many hours making models that illustrate mathematical ideas. 'They really give you a feel for the idea', he would say. Indeed, it is as if the idea of observing and constructing are cyclical from his point of view — observe and construct, then observe again, and reconstruct. Under pressure from the time constraints of syllabus and testing, perhaps we do not allow enough time for children to observe and construct for themselves.

MAKING MODELS

Children can learn a great deal from making their own learning aids. For example, number facts can be learned with the help of models, which the children construct for themselves.

One class of 7-year-olds had decided it was time for them to stop worrying about addition and to learn their number facts once and for all. With the children we drew up a table for addition, and spent some time looking for strategies that might help learning. We wondered if a construction approach might help and asked the children how Lego bricks and a base board might help. The children started to build a representation of the table, and soon got a different kind of feel for statements such as,

'To get to $6+7$, think of $6+6$, then add one.'

as they were able to observe and track the statement on their constructions.

MAKING A KITE

Observation is an essential part of some model-making activities. Making a kite provides good opportunities for this.

On another occasion a Year 7 teacher brought his kite to school to fly at lunchtime. Many Year 5, 6, and 7 children saw this as a challenge to make their own kites. A group of four 10-year-old boys took this very seriously and before beginning to make their own kites, carried out thorough research on the topic. The children monitored the variety of kites that other children were now flying at lunchtimes. These kites were based on designs suggested by parents and grandparents who had been quizzed about how they made kites as children. The group also went to the library and researched the history and design of kites. They discussed the types of materials available and tested some for strength. They continued to observe the different types of kite that hovered over the lunchtime playground, and discussed the merits of each of the shapes under different wind conditions. As the boys collected all this information they made copious notes and sketches. They collected so much information that they didn't know how to deal with it. Their class teacher wondered if they would ever make and fly a kite.

In discussion, the boys explained their predicament to the teacher who responded by showing them how information can be organised on a matrix. The boys adopted this idea and made their own table, with headings such as, 'Lift-off', 'How much wind?' etc. Then one morning, in came the boys with a diamond-shaped kite, almost the same size as they were, made out of a plastic bag and garden stakes. When asked why this (almost unbelievably simple, unadorned kite) was the chosen design, the boys used their matrix to support the following reasoning,

'Well, the diamond kites seem to lift off easily.'

'Yeah, they fly in any wind too!'

'Polythene was the strongest and lightest material.'

'And it sort of fills out with the wind. Phil's Grandad always used brown paper but brown paper stays stiff and flat.'

When asked if they were satisfied with their results, Grant replied,

'Yes, but now we're designing and trying different launching methods.'

On completion of this project, a simple book was published showing how to make their kite, and discussing how best to launch it. What materials and how much of each to use, size and how to scale it up or down were also detailed.

In this example we see how important it can be to allow time for children, who are possibly unsure of what to do, to observe a situation as a way of understanding it. It was also very important for the group of four to actually construct and test their preferred design. For many children, the process of construction is equally important as this can be their most effective way of representing the solution that they have arrived at.

DIAGRAMMING AND INTERPRETING

Diagrams are a vital part of expressing mathematical ideas, not only those geometric constructions, drawn with ruler and compass, but also rough diagrams that serve as organisers for subsequent thinking. Diagrams can help children to:

- build bridges between intuitive ideas and formal mathematics;

- make quick records of ideas and information;

- visualise aspects of a problem;

- organise and interpret information that they have collected;

- summarise information to explain a solution.

TREASURE HUNT CHARTS

A large-scale, accurate map can be used for a treasure hunt, where the clues encourage the children to locate features of the map.

A group of 6- and 7-year-olds who had been particularly enthralled by the class theme of pirates wanted to bury some treasure and make a treasure hunt for the rest of the class to follow. Having decided to hold the treasure hunt outside, Harry, Sharon, Monika and Brendan went out to try to plan a route. They each made a rough picture map of their school grounds and marked the places that they thought would be good spots to hide clues.

Back in a corner of the classroom they discovered that their maps were all very different. They discussed, even argued about where things actually were, what was missing from various maps and what it was silly to mark on a map. It was Monika who said,

'Suppose the cars aren't all there when we have the treasure hunt.'

Brendan agreed,

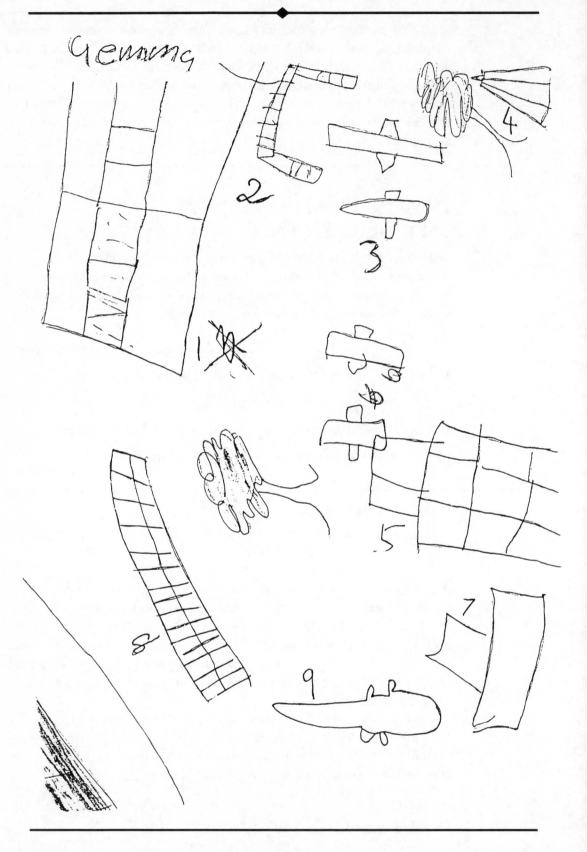

'Yes! They park in different places. Who comes first chooses first!'

They tried copying the information from all of the maps onto one map. This didn't work either.

Finally they decided that the only way to do it was to go back outside now that they knew what to mark and what not to mark, and to work together to make one good map. This was their final draft which was 'polished' back in the classroom. Together they made one or two alterations, coloured it in, marked the sequence for the route and made up the clues. After a very successful treasure hunt, this group, with the aid of the teacher, made up a wall chart detailing the stages of planning and making a treasure hunt.

The children in this example had drawn rough diagrams. They knew a diagram was needed but not exactly what information it needed to show. When they put their diagrams together, they began to realise that different information was needed and also a more detailed way of showing it. The first attempt at a diagram frequently has shortcomings: it may not relate exactly to the problem, it may present inappropriate information or it may present information in a way that is not easy to interpret. That is not to say that the diagram has not served a useful purpose, rather that, as in this example, the diagram has helped the problem solver to see more clearly:

- what the problem is;
- what information is required;
- how best to present that information.

The result is a more clearly defined view of the information actually needed and the most efficient way of presenting it.

As the children worked on their maps, they were in fact interpreting information at a variety of levels. They:

- went out collecting and interpreting information around the school;
- developed an understanding of what a map is for and what information it needs to show;
- compared maps and identified omissions and unwanted information;
- combined each other's plans to make one accurate map.

They weren't the only ones to benefit from this activity either. The rest of the class now had a real reason for interpreting information from a map, as they tried to follow the clues and find the treasure.

GENERATING DATA AND DRAWING CONCLUSIONS

Whether working on an investigation such as,

$1 \times 3 - 1 =$
$2 \times 4 - 1 =$
$3 \times 5 - 1 =$

Explore and Explain

or developing an understanding of a particular mathematical concept, children frequently need to generate data from which they can draw conclusions. As with the earlier examples that we have given in this chapter, children's first attempts may need rethinking or refining, or their information may need reorganising to show a clear result.

DISCOVERING π

Assorted objects that roll can be used to provide the information needed to investigate the existence and value of π.

After working with a class of 11-year-olds who were confident with decimals and used the calculator as an aid whenever they felt the need of it, we thought it would be worth trying a new way of introducing them to pi. We asked them to bring to school 'something round, like a bottle or tin', and the class came good with a variety of sizes. At the start of the maths lesson, the question came,

'What're all these bottles for?'

'Well,' we said, 'we've a challenge for you. Get into groups of three or four, and pick four different containers for your group. Then see if you can estimate how many turns each one will make in rolling exactly 1 metre.'

After the groups had made their estimates, there was general surprise when they came to check by actually rolling the containers. When we asked the class to share what, if anything, they had found out, it was clear that most children thought that a larger container would be associated with a larger number of turns. The information that they had generated caused them to consider and compare the results with their earlier estimates. It was Alice who then suggested a new idea,

'The big bottles don't take so many turns as the little ones.'

As there seemed to be general agreement with this new principle, we asked the groups if they wanted to find their own reasons for this and whether they could use their reasoning to make better estimates.

Most of the groups tried measuring the width of their containers and experimenting with addition and subtraction. At the next report back, it was clear that a little more input from us was required,

> 'Well, you've measured your containers and you've tried adding and subtracting. Is there anything else you could do?'

Returning to their places, the children tried what multiplication and division would show. Soon they wanted to share their results. Alice asked if we could put everyone's answers together '. . . in one big table'. She supplied the headings, and the rest of the class supplied the data.

The numbers in the table prompted the children to ask for more accuracy. For example, Group B was required to check its measurements (now five), and all counting of 'How many turns?' was redone with a view to getting closer results. The process of generating accurate information was by now well under way.

This was the first of a series of experiments that we as teachers used to encourage the children to generate data from which they could draw conclusions about the constant π. Our approach was, if you like, that of conceptual drafting, offering the children opportunities to make closer and closer approximations in their move towards an understanding of π — both as a constant factor, and as a particular value.

In this example the children generated data to check their estimates. The information collected required them to rethink their estimates. The conclusions that they drew from the data they had collected resulted in:

- the children seeing a relationship between containers, radius and the number of rolls required to cover 1 metre;
- the children carrying out an investigation into why this was so.

The investigation of course required the generation of more data, data that the children soon realised had to be very accurately collected if it was to be useful. After presenting their data on a chart the children were able to draw firm conclusions about the relationship of the radius to the number of turns it would require.

In one class of 12-year-olds two groups were working on the same investigation (as it happened a group of boys and a group of girls).

ON THE DIAGONAL

Draw a rectangle on squared paper and draw the diagonal.
How many squares of the paper does the diagonal pass through?
Try this for other rectangles. What do you notice?

The girls began drawing lots of different rectangles after deciding to work together. They quickly generated information about a variety of rectangles. They questioned each other about the number of squares passed through in each case but couldn't follow and keep track of them all. They thought a table would help them to keep track of all their findings but as you can see from the disorganised array of figures it was still not possible to draw any conclusions from the information. Their class teacher reminded them of an earlier problem that they'd tackled when it was important to be systematic, and left them to think about this. The girls then set about reorganising the information they had already collected, but still not clear conclusions could be drawn. Finally Debra asked,

'Have we got enough information? We don't have all the one rectangles or the two rectangles and so on!'

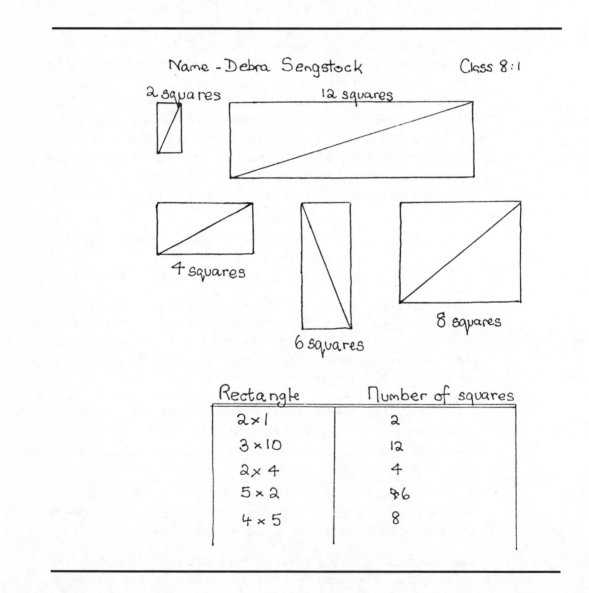

Name - Debra Sengstock   Class 8:1

2 squares   12 squares

4 squares

6 squares

8 squares

Rectangle	Number of squares
2 × 1	2
3 × 10	12
2 × 4	4
5 × 2	~~7~~6
4 × 5	8

The figure shows their final and effective way of generating and recording information. At last a conclusion could be drawn.

Like the girls, the boys began to draw rectangles, marking on the diagonals and counting the squares passed through. They were working independently but stopped to compare results quite early on. Their random sampling had generated a very clear conclusion, or so the boys thought, for each of their diagonals had passed through one more square than the number of squares along the shorter edge of each rectangle. The boys were asked to generate more information to check that their theory always worked. For a while it did and then they generated examples that did not fit their conclusion. Their first response was to try to spot defects or inaccuracies in the diagonals,

'We mustn't have gone corner to corner exactly. That must be it.'

It was hard work persuading the boys that they needed to generate more data systematically before they tried to draw more conclusions. After each three or four rectangles the boys impatiently looked for patterns or rules and were constantly sidetracked to pursue other rules on the basis of only one or two examples. They were drawing conclusions without generating data on which to base them, e.g.,

'You times the L by the B, and take something away.'

'You add one on each time.'

'You add then take away, add then take away!'

Finally the boys went to see what the girls were doing. A quick look at their diagrams sent the boys back to try that themselves. Each of their rules was confirmed as they systematically worked through each set of rectangles, but none of the rules worked for all the rectangles. Now they knew why it was necessary to generate, systematically in this case, enough data to be able to see clearly what was going on and draw informal conclusions.

THE COMMON THREAD

The focus of this chapter has been 'working it out'. In essence, this means having ideas, trying them out, and revising them in the light of findings and comments from others. Two important mathematical processes are at work here:

- *generalising* — where we try to make general statements (or hypotheses) about situations;
- *specialising* — where we collect particular items of information that provide special cases of more general situations.

For example, a class project might start from the generalisation,

'Anything boys can do girls can do just as well.'

To test this statement, the project invites the children to think of ways in which they might collect particular or 'special' information (e.g. from their class or age group) with which to test whether this statement is fair. In this situation a generalisation can be tested by specialising; in other contexts, however, specialising may be the first step, as it provides information for a generalisation to be based on.

When the conclusion to a problem is reached, it is seldom accurate to describe the process that led up to the solution in terms of the understanding that we now have. Or, to put it another way, hindsight is a poor tool to use to describe the thinking process. Edward de Bono, in a talk based on *The Mechanism of the Mind*, described the difference between going forward and looking back.

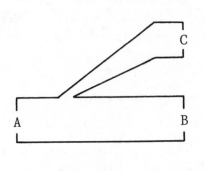

Thinking about a problem is depicted as the broad path, **AB**. The narrow gap in the path that leads to the solution, **C**, is hard to find if you are on the path. But once at **C**, the reverse track **CA** is simple to follow. Since most of our time on a mathematical journey is spent on paths such as **AB**, it is important to reflect this in how we teach. Recording, even respecting, only the narrow path of hindsight, **CA**, is to ignore the process of mathematical activity. But enough of this theorising, let us turn to some further examples of young mathematicians at work and see what happens when the process approach is encouraged.

♦

3

CHILDREN

COMMUNICATING

Talking/Listening   *Writing/Reading*   *Reporting/Reacting*
Discussing

In the first part of this chapter we will be looking at what happens when children are given opportunities to communicate at all stages of their work. In Chapter 1 we looked specifically at children discussing their way into a problem or activity. We build on this here, looking at:

- children talking on the job;
- children using the language they feel comfortable with;
- children talking their way to understanding;
- children reporting to others;
- children using illustrations, diagrams, models and symbols to support their reports;
- children using illustrations, diagrams, models or symbols alone to convey their messages;
- children reacting to other children's communications.

The final section of this chapter looks at discussion as a special form of communication in the maths classroom.

The now well-researched fields of language acquisition and process writing have shown that by the time children come to school they are able to use language in purposeful situations to communicate their ideas, needs and emotions to others. They are able to use this language to describe, explain, persuade, plan and tell stories using appropriate vocabulary and language structures. The process writing approach encourages the children to continue to play with words, explore language patterns and structures, invent, approximate and make mistakes as they draft and redraft their own stories. At every stage of the writing process, children communicate with each other, the teacher or some other agency, thinking their way into their topic, discussing to develop new skills and strategies, discovering aspects that need changing or correcting. They do all this with confidence, knowing that their attempts and mistakes are valued.

In maths lessons, children do not necessarily have similar expectations or experiences of trying to master mathematical language to communicate ideas, needs or emotions. In fact, for many, mathematics is neither purposeful nor a means of communication. As teachers, we must ensure that children will have a need to communicate mathematical ideas and develop the appropriate vocabulary, structures and conventions needed for this, but how? We worked with teachers to provide an environment where the children were encouraged to share ideas, skills, strategies and results with others. To do this the children were encouraged to:

- have discussions and listen carefully to others;
- express their ideas in their own natural language as a bridge towards using more formal mathematical language;
- be receptive and supportive to each other;
- present ideas, discoveries and findings to others in as many media as possible (orally, in writing, using models, illustrations, diagrams and symbols as appropriate);
- react to reports by asking questions, confirming ideas or methods, extending or innovating on the ideas presented;
- discuss their ideas and their work with each other and with the teacher, individually, as part of a group and occasionally as a whole class.

In this environment we observed children confidently using their own natural language, making mistakes, and working towards closer approximations of mathematical language. For us, this highlighted the fact that children do not become competent users of mathematical ideas and language overnight. Rather, they move forward to increasing competency with mathematical language over longer periods of time as they use, experiment with and communicate their mathematical ideas. This is something that is rarely considered in most maths classrooms. Providing a variety of contexts in which the children had something to communicate, for example, designing, planning and making activities, resulted in the need for children to communicate. They had ideas, pictures and models that they needed to support with explanations and descriptions. In many instances the children talked themselves into understanding, changing their pictures, models and ideas as they thought out loud.

TALKING AND LISTENING

FREE GROUPING

Give each group some shape pieces to sort in any way that they decide. Encourage the children to talk about what they are doing.

Quite spontaneously one morning, Bobbi, Fiva and Dennis, who were sitting at the sorting table, decided that they would sort out bits to use to make houses. Even before they began to construct, the need to communicate, to explore thoughts about how to begin, led straight into the use of natural language peppered with some mathematical terms — triangle, straight, square — that were currently being explored in more formal contexts.

Bobbi: 'Straight bits!'

Fiva looked puzzled,

'Not for the roof though?'

Bobbi demonstrated how to make a roof and as she did so she said,

'A triangle for the roof needs three bits, look.'

Dennis looked over, pointed and said in a questioning tone,

'Triangle?'

Fiva and Bobbi just nodded,

Fiva: 'A house needs a door and a handle [as he looked for appropriate bits]. Good, a circle for a handle...too big.'

Quietly now the pieces were being assembled. Having made his outline, Dennis began sorting long, flat strips.

Dennis: 'I want long ones.'

Bobbi: 'What are they for?'

Dennis [looking surprised]: 'For walls.'

Bobbi: 'I'm going to use shells for flowers.'

Dennis looked at her for a while, thinking, then not to be outdone, said,

'I'm making a square chimney with smoke coming out.'

Fiva: 'You've filled it in. What can I use to fill mine in?'

When we reflect on what was actually going on as these children were talking and listening, we see that:

- the children, though at times only thinking out loud, were being listened to by others and were also being positively responded to;
- ideas were being exchanged and built on, adapted or extended by others;
- peer group tutoring was going on — Dennis learned about a triangle and Fiva was challenged to take his house design one step further.

Not only did the children talk about what they were going to do, they later showed their products to their friends, explaining what they had done. A few days later the photographs shown on pages 44 and 46 were used to make a poster for the Maths Interest Centre, with the children's captions written beneath, creating a permanent record for all to see, use as inspiration, or reflect on.

This example clearly shows what linguists have described as the difference between competence and performance. Children have a much wider vocabulary than they generally demonstrate. They understand a wide range of words long before they begin to use them in their speech. This is true of mathematical language too. Children seem to need to hear a word in many different contexts before it becomes part of their natural and spontaneous vocabulary, which is perhaps what happened to Dennis. The converse is also true. In settings where children feel secure, they will often try out a new term, testing it out in a new situation. This seems less common in the classroom than in the more comfortable family setting and peer groups outside the classroom.

Bobbi, Dennis and Fiva, in their discussion about sorting and constructing, also tried out some of the terms they had been hearing the teacher use. Dennis, for whom English was a second language, was supported in his developing language and was confident knowing that his house was admired and copied.

LIMITING THE CHARACTERISTICS

Collections of objects for sorting by one or two characteristics can be used to focus on particular aspects of measurement, shape or comparison, e.g.,

length   strips of paper, fabric, card, wood, string, straws, pattern blocks

shape   counters, mosaic tiles, pattern blocks, Lego, cartons, bottletops

On another occasion the teacher spent some time with Dennis trying to develop the language, 'big, bigger, biggest'. At first Dennis could not find words to describe his picture of the elephants, shown below. The teacher supplied the terms 'big', 'bigger', 'biggest' and worked with Dennis until he could use these comparative terms to describe his picture. She then encouraged Dennis to show and talk about his picture with other children, expecting him to use his new vocabulary. Again, Dennis began to struggle to find terms to describe it and then slowly and hesitantly he said,

'Giant elephant, big elephant, small elephant.'

Pleased with himself, he asked to have this written on his picture. Dennis really wanted to talk about his picture; he was not being difficult by not using the comparative terms, 'big, bigger, biggest'. He was probably not yet comfortable with those terms or confident enough to use them, or maybe 'giant' expressed better the way he felt about the biggest elephant. He was certainly satisfied with the message that he did communicate and the other children were certainly impressed by the idea of a 'giant elephant', wanting to know more about it.

A HEALTHY DIET

Handouts from sources such as a doctor's waiting room can be used by the children to understand their diet and plan for healthy eating.

Sometimes children are given or choose a problem or activity that they do not fully understand. This is what happened to the group using the 'Foods rich in dietary fibre' chart. They were having real problems understanding what it meant.

Lai was the first to start talking out loud,

Lai: 'What does "portion and wt" mean?'

Tammy: 'Yeah, and why does it say g stroke 100 g?'

Seni: 'It's like e.g. and etc. I think.'

Sam: 'I've got it. It's short for weight.'

They all looked down the column saying the numbers out loud.

Lai: 'These must be grams.'

Tammy: 'What about this other one then?'

Seni: 'What are the numbers for under that? What do they mean?'

Lai: 'Look at the numbers in the next column. Look...they're smaller. They're how much you get in one biscuit...see.'

Tammy: 'Ah...[a ray of hope], these are how much in a packet...so...g/100g must mean how much grams of fibre...in...100.'

Comfortable now, the children felt ready to interpret the information on the chart and later deliberately used the abbreviations in their report to the rest of the class. Their looks of achievement when asked by the class to explain the abbreviations and how they knew what they meant told a story of its own.

By working together, asking questions, thinking out loud, listening to each other's half-formed ideas, this group was able to struggle towards

Foods rich in dietary fibre

Food Source	Portion (Wt.)	Total Dietary Fibre (g/100g)	Total Dietary Fibre Per Portion	Food Source	Portion (Wt.)	Total Dietary Fibre (g/100g)	Total Dietary Fibre Per Portion
Biscuits				Nectarines	1 med	2.40	2.40
Fully coated				Olives in brine	1 med	4.40	0.38
Chocolate	1 biscuit (16.6)	3.09	0.51	Oranges	1 med	2.00	4.00
Crispbread–Rye	1 biscuit (8.9)	11.37	1.01	Passionfruit	1 med	15.90	7.95
Crispbread–				Peaches	1 med	1.40	1.54
Wheat	1 biscuit (5.9)	4.83	0.28	Pears	1 med	1.70	3.40
Ginger	1 biscuit (8.9)	1.99	0.18	Plums	1 med	2.10	1.05
Matzo	1 biscuit (18.75)	3.85	0.72	Prunes	150g	16.10	24.15
Sandwich biscuit	1 biscuit (22.7)	1.20	0.27	Sultanas	small pack	7.00	2.80
Semi sweet	1 biscuit (8.3)	2.31	0.20	**Nuts**			
Shortbread	1 biscuit (12.5)	2.10	0.26	Brazil	150g	9.00	13.50
Water	1 biscuit (2.6)	3.20	0.08	Peanuts	150g	8.10	12.15
Filled wafer	1 biscuit (7.4)	1.62	0.11	**Pastry**			
Bread				Flaky cooked	1 slice (25)	2.00	0.50
Brown	1 slice (27.2)	5.11	1.39	Shortcrust	1 slice (25)	2.40	0.60
Hi–Fibre Brown	1 slice (27.2)	9.50	2.58	**Preserves**			
Hi–Fibre White	1 slice (27.2)	7.60	2.07	Chutney	teaspoon	1.80	0.09
White	1 slice (27.2)	2.72	0.74	Jam–strawberry	teaspoon		
Wholemeal	1 slice (27.2)	8.50	2.31	–blackberry	teaspoon	1.10	0.05
Bread rolls				Marmalade	teaspoon	0.71	0.03
Crusty Brown	1 roll (75)	5.90	4.42	Pickle	teaspoon	1.53	0.08
Soft Brown	1 roll (75)	5.40	4.05	Plum jam	teaspoon	0.93	0.05
Crusty White	1 roll (75)	3.10	2.32	Peanut butter	teaspoon	7.60	0.38
Soft White	1 roll (75)	2.90	2.17	**Vegetables**			
Cakes				Asparagus boiled	av. serve	1.50	2.25
Cheese cake	1 slice (62.5)	0.90	0.56	Beans–french–			
Fancy Iced	1 slice (62.5)	2.40	1.50	boiled	av. serve	3.20	4.80
Lemon Meringue pie	1 slice (62.5)	0.70	0.44	Beans–broad–			
Pancakes	1 pancake (125)	0.90	1.12	boiled	av. serve	3.40	5.10
Rich Fruit cake	1 slice (57.1)	3.50	2.00	Beans baked in			
Sponge cake	1 slice (43.75)	1.00	0.44	tomato sauce	av. serve	7.30	9.49
Sponge jam filled	1 slice (43.75)	1.20	0.53	Beansprouts–			
Cereals				canned	av. serve	3.00	4.50
All-Bran	1 bowl (60)	26.70	16.02	Broccoli–tops			
Bran	1 bowl (60)	44.00	26.40	boiled	av. serve	4.10	6.15
Cornflakes	1 bowl (60)	1.40	0.84	Brussels sprouts			
Muesli	1 bowl (60)	7.41	4.45	boiled	av. serve	2.90	4.35
Porridge	1 bowl (60)	0.24	0.14	Cabbage (spring)			
Puffed Wheat	1 bowl (60)	15.41	9.25	boiled	av. serve	2.20	3.30
Rice	1 bowl (60)	2.40	1.44	Carrots–boiled	av. serve	3.10	4.65
Shredded wheat	1 bowl (60)	12.26	7.36	–raw	2 small	2.90	4.35
Special K	1 bowl (60)	5.54	3.32	Cauliflower–boiled	av. serve	1.80	2.70
Weetbix	1 bowl (60)	12.72	7.63	Celery–raw	2 storks	1.80	2.70
Flours				Cucumber	1 med	0.40	1.20
Brown	100g	7.87	7.87	Lettuce	med head	1.50	10.50
Soya full fat	100g	11.90	11.90	Marrow–cooked	av. serve	0.60	0.90
Soya low fat	100g	14.30	14.30	Mushrooms–fried	av. serve	4.00	6.00
White plain	100g	3.40	3.40	–raw	15 med	2.50	3.75
White S.R.	100g	3.70	3.70	Onions–fried	av. serve	4.50	6.75
White				–raw	2 med	1.30	1.95
Breadmaking	100g	3.15	3.15	Spring onions–raw	bunch	3.10	3.87
Wholemeal	100g	9.51	9.51	Parsley–raw	bunch	9.10	6.82
Fruit				Parsnips–boiled	av. serve	5.20	3.75
Apples–fresh only	1 med	1.42	2.84	Peas–boiled	av. serve	6.30	9.45
Apples–peel only	1	3.71	7.42	–canned	av. serve	7.75	11.62
Apricots–fresh				–frozen (raw)	av. serve	0.50	0.75
and skin	1 med	2.10	1.05	Radishes	bunch	1.00	3.00
Raw apricots (dried)	100g	24.00	24.00	Spinach–boiled	av. serve	6.30	9.45
Stewed apricots	150g	8.50	12.75	Sweetcorn–boiled			
Avocado pears	1 med	2.00	5.00	(on-the-cob)	1 cob	1.50	2.25
Bananas	1 med	3.40	5.10	Tomatoes–canned	av. serve	0.90	1.35
Cherries	150g	1.70	2.55	–raw	2 small	1.50	2.25
Currants	150g	8.70	13.05	**Potatoes**			
Dates dried	150g	8.70	13.05	Baked	3 small	2.50	5.00
Fruit salad (canned)	150g	1.10	1.65	Boiled	3 small	1.00	2.00
Grapes black	150g	0.40	0.60	Canned	3 small	2.50	5.00
Grapes white	150g	0.90	1.35	Crisps	small pack	11.90	2.97
Grapefruit–raw	1 med	0.60	2.70	Fried chips	av. serve	3.20	4.80
Lemons–whole	1 med	5.20	5.72	Mashed	av. serve	0.90	1.80
Melons–raw							
Canteloupe	½ med	11.00	49.50				

Adapted from Southgate DAT. Bailey B. Collinson E Et al: J Human Nutrition 30:303. 1976.

an understanding of the chart, one child's partly formed idea often being accepted and built on by another as they talked their way into an understanding of the situation. Of course the long silences and time taken to reach this understanding could have been done away with if the teacher had just told them what it all meant, but then what would they have learned, achieved or later remembered?

WRITING AND READING

An often neglected form of communication in the maths lesson is that of writing. Any writing and reading that does go on tends to be part of the construction of charts, tables, graphs or in a symbolic form. The role of writing as a way of exploring ideas, understanding and attitudes is a largely unexplored aspect of maths. Here we take a broad view of writing and reading, referring to making marks on paper as writing and interpreting marks on papers as reading. This enables us to include drawings, sketches, doodles and cartoons, as well as number stories, reports, journal entries, captions, diagrams and symbols, under this broad umbrella.

The advantages already shown for oral communication also apply to written forms of communication, as the following examples show.

ILLUSTRATING NUMBERS

Encourage the children to draw groups of different sizes and label their group. Allow them to choose their own numbers and forms of illustration.

Sitting in a group one day, Darryl said,

'I'm going to draw ten dogs.'

Bobbi said,

'Well I'm going to draw four people.'

Fiva topped them both with,

'I'm going to draw 14.'

The drawing, colouring and counting began. Darryl very easily and quickly drew his ten dogs and moved on to another table. Fiva was having trouble. He would draw one picture and then count one more, and then count again and so on until he had too many to count without getting lost. Quietly he wrote the numbers 1–14 across the top of his page. It did not help. After a quiet period he picked up a felt pen and wrote the numbers in the things he had already drawn and continued

to mark each one until he had reached fourteen. Satisfied with himself now he crossed out the numbers at the top of the page. Fiva had written his way to understanding.

Bobbi, too, had to use written numerals to help her. After slowly and meticulously drawing her four tiny figures, Fiva said to her,

'You said you were going to draw four people. Can't you count?'

Bobbi sulked, looking at her paper for a long time before looking at Fiva's and seeing his row of numerals. She wrote the numbers 1–20 along the top of her page and then got the idea of numbering the items on her page, talking out loud as she did so,

'One people, two people, three people...four...three people and the dog makes four.'

At this point she picked up her pink felt pen and wrote a large confident 4 beside her row of people and the dog. Then she turned to Fiva and said again,

'Three people and the dog makes four.'

By numbering not in sequence but first the people and then the dog, she had found a solution to Fiva's comment that suited her. Talking alone would not have helped her; it was the numbers she wrote that clarified her thinking.

Children are beginning to expect to write for an audience in process writing classrooms. They also expect to read what other children have read. By having an audience in mind, children begin to adapt their writing style and the content of their writing to suit.

We have found that children can do this in mathematics too. Children enjoy the challenge of making workcards for others to use, which engages them in all stages of process writing. They have ideas about the content and the skills/concepts to be practised. They generate instructions and examples to which they have to find correct answers. They show them to others for comment and then refine or change them. They work out a design for their workcard and an answer card that will appeal to others and then 'publish' their end product.

Children can also be encouraged to write instructions for other children to use, for example, instructions for making a model or mathematical game. Instructions, as you will know if you have ever tried, are very difficult to write clearly and succinctly. This is not a reason why children should not write instructions, rather it is a reason why they should do so. By trying to write instructions, children become more sensitive to the way instructions are written, sequenced, and illustrated when they come to read or follow them elsewhere. Children can become very inventive when faced with the need to communicate how to do something as can be seen in the next activity.

CHILDREN COMMUNICATING

TUCKSHOP ORDERS

Encourage a group of children to take responsibility for organising the class tuckshop order. They could compile the order, collect the right money and distribute the goods.

Each week one group in a Year 5 class was responsible for collecting and recording tuckshop orders and money. Apparently, every group always listed each item separately so, for example, potato chips would appear on a list seven or eight times, making the checking of totals very difficult. A group of very reluctant boys, who apparently hated reading and writing, began to streamline the job. After noticing that they had written 'orange popper, orange popper, orange popper' on this list, Troy crossed two of them off and put three ticks beside the one left. They adopted this approach for the rest of the orders that day but by next day they had been to the tuckshop and listed all the items for sale and the price of each. A simple tally system had now been arrived at that made recording orders and, more importantly, reading the orders, very quick. As the children were working out how much money they should have collected, they recorded all their amounts, e.g.,

'Six at 12 cents = 72 cents.'

Martin, inspired by all this, listed all the prices and made the following table.

Tuck Shop Orders

		1	2	3	4	5	6	7
pies	90c	90	1.80	2.70	3.60	4.50	5.40	6.30
ham san	80c	80	1.60	2.40	3.20	4.00	4.80	5.60
cheese san	60c	60	1.20	1.80	2.40	3.00	3.60	4.20
vegemite san	40c	40	80	1.20	1.60	2.00	2.40	2.80
popcorn	30c	30	60	90	1.20	1.50	1.80	2.10
health bars	30c	30	60	90	1.20	1.50	1.80	2.10
milk	30c	30	60	90	1.20	1.50	1.80	2.10
poppers	60c	60	1.20	1.80	2.40	3.00	3.60	4.20
fruit	35c	35	70	1.05	1.40	1.75	2.10	2.45
ice blocks	12c	12	24	36	48	60	72	84

53

He said nothing as he was doing it and then thrust it at Troy. Troy looked at it blankly before light dawned and he said,

'It's one of them multiplication things...one times 12 cents is 12, two times 12 cents is 24 cents.'

Writing and reading on the job had greatly streamlined the chore of collecting tuckshop money and orders. The tuckshop workers were delighted with the tally system and copied the idea so that every class could send in their orders in this clear way.

KEEPING A JOURNAL

Regular entries in children's personal maths journals can include:

- methods and strategies they have tried,
- problems they have met and solutions they have found,
- items of personal interest,
- feelings towards a topic.

Writing and reading have an extra dimension that talking doesn't. They make possible the expression of personal ideas in private. We have encouraged children to turn to their own personal journals at any time in the maths lesson, and particularly at the end of a lesson, to record how they feel about the work they are doing, to ask questions, record insights or strategies, to doodle and roughly work something out. At first children of all ages find this extremely difficult, and write only simple comments like,

'I hate algebra.'

'I like times.'

Over time, however, children turn more and more to their journals. Renee had been in school for almost two years drawing pictures but using almost no recognisable letters or numbers. All the children in her class had a maths journal in which they could illustrate, record, or write as they used concrete materials in the maths lessons. Renee had used her book to draw in, always writing her name at the top, until one day Marilyn said she just wanted to practise her numbers. Renee watched and then began slowly and deliberately forming numbers too. She looked at a number poster on the wall and copied the five, trying to draw five apples beside it. She tried the three and then the five again. For days, Renee just sat and wrote strings of numbers in her journal until one day she said to her teacher,

'I can write numbers you know.' [She showed her book.] 'Can I have another book?'

We include this example because it highlights something that we, as teachers, tend to forget — that children need to be allowed to practise a skill, working on it in their own way, in their own time, when they are interested. Her teacher had tried many times and in many different ways to teach Renee to write numerals. Renee, when she was ready, quickly and efficiently taught herself. Her first attempts quickly became closer approximations to properly formed numerals.

Mark, a very timid 8-year-old, was working with a group of children who were trying to estimate which things around the room were 20 centimetres long. Mark would not take a risk in front of the group and refused to participate until his teacher suggested that he write down all the objects in his journal rather than say them out loud. She told Mark he would not have to show anyone unless he wanted to. Writing just for himself, Mark was happy to carry out the activity and to take risks. Later when he realised that most of his estimates were quite close he let the rest of the group read his results. For Mark, writing in the journal was like writing for a trusted friend as it offered him the support he needed.

A Year 5 class who had been keeping maths journals for almost a term had begun to use them to record what they had learnt in a lesson. After a lesson on co-ordinates, Joe made the following entry:

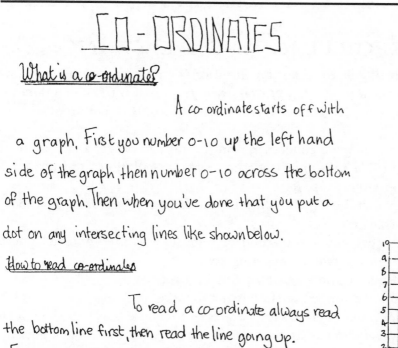

CO-ORDINATES

What is a co-ordinate?

A co-ordinate starts off with a graph. First you number 0-10 up the left hand side of the graph, then number 0-10 across the bottom of the graph. Then when you've done that you put a dot on any intersecting lines like shown below.

How to read co-ordinates

To read a co-ordinate always read the bottom line first, then read the line going up. For example :- look down at the bottom picture

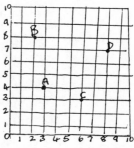

A = (3,4)
B = (2,8)
C = (6,3)
D = (8,7)

He had developed a very concise and precise way of recording after each lesson and was often asked by children sitting near him to read what he had written so they could see if they had forgotten anything. Joe's teacher said that since he had developed this style of writing in his journal his maths work had really improved and so had his confidence. Now when she asked,

'Do you remember the work we did on...?'

Joe would flick through his journal, skim quickly through what he had written and remember exactly what they had done.

The few examples given here highlight the range of different types of writing about maths that children can be encouraged to engage in. Writing, like talking, can help to clarify thinking, to convey messages to others, but it also has the special quality of being permanent. It can be referred to later for revision of a skill or concept or to see how one's thinking and understanding have changed. Writing, too, can be edited and refined or made more precise as new information and understandings develop. Writing can be shared many times with many different audiences, which means that it is a very different form of communication than the oral mode. As such, it should become a constant feature of maths lessons.

REPORTING AND REACTING

Reporting is an important form of communication in mathematics. Reports, whether they be oral, written, with or without diagrams, drawings or models, are a key way of ensuring that children:

- talk or write coherently and formally to others about their work;
- provide substance (measurements, calculations, statistics) to support their reports;
- explain how their solutions were arrived at, sharing methods and strategies;
- discuss why one method or resource was used and not another;
- hear a range of reporting styles;
- listen to and question items in a report;
- confirm or refute statements made;
- meet new methods and strategies to realise that there can be many ways to find an answer and that there is not always one right answer;
- try out and adopt other people's mathematical ideas and strategies.

BELONGS, DOESN'T BELONG

One player thinks of a rule and the other players try to find the rule by thinking of numbers that belong to it. For example, if the rule is 'multiples of 3' and these guesses were made:

1, 4, 9, 5, 25, 16, 6, 2, 18, ...

the following table would show the guesses so far and the order in which they were generated:

Belongs			9	6	18	...
Doesn't Belong			1	5	2	
			4	25		
				16		

Christopher and Debbie had become really involved in finding rules and patterns, for the game 'Belongs, Doesn't Belong'. For more than a week they generated unusual rules and patterns to try out on the class. They used Unifix cubes to find out as much as they could about making patterns and rules and asked the teacher if they could organise a game for the class. The teacher agreed on the condition that they report on their week's research to the rest of the class after the game. Christopher and Debbie gave their report but in very bald terms,

> Debbie: 'We found out about prime numbers. Prime numbers are numbers like 5, 7, er...11, ... It's your turn now, Chris.'

> Christopher: 'We found square numbers and triangular numbers. We don't know if there are oblong numbers yet. We're doing them next.'

As Christopher and Debbie gave their report there were many confused faces and the other children were not really attending. The teacher asked the class if they had any questions. There was no response so she asked,

> Teacher: 'Do you know what a square number is?'

> Class: 'No.'

> Teacher: 'Well, you do have a question then, don't you?'

The class seemed to realise that it was all right not to know and began to ask questions. Christopher and Debbie, on the spot, began to report and explain more fully what they had done — how they had used Unifix to help them, what they had discovered and how the teacher had provided the terms they did not know so that they could describe their rules and patterns. Time was set aside for the rest of the class, now very interested, to try these out for themselves.

We have used this example of a poorly formed report to demonstrate the following points. Firstly, that children do not have many opportunities in school to report on their work, and, as a result, do not know what a report is and what should be in it. Secondly, to show that peer reaction soon demands that a report be smartened up. The questions left unanswered help the children to focus on what should be included in a report, and last, but not least, to show how a report can be reacted to in more than one way. In this case, initial response was negative, followed by a series of questions and then a positive response resulting in action. We believe, and have frequently observed, that children quickly and readily develop the 'report' genre, ordering, structuring and including only the important information. The sifting through, classifying and sequencing process necessary in the process of formalising a report is an essential part of the learning process. The children reflect on what they have done and what they have discovered as they do so. Reports, then, need not be just the summary of an activity, they can also be the stimulus for much more activity.

DISCUSSING

The conference approach to reading and writing has brought about changes in classroom organisation. During a conference or discussion, children communicate their ideas, results or problems with other children, the teacher, or both. Discussions are most commonly used when the teacher or children identify the need for a new skill or strategy, or need a sounding board for their ideas or problems. During a discussion, the children soon realise how important it is not just to talk, but to listen, respond and share.

Discussions have equal value in the maths lesson too. Often the whole class does not progress at the same pace and one group may need a particular mathematical skill or concept session to solve a problem. Another might have just discovered something interesting and need guidance on how to pursue it. Discussions help teachers to cope with this. Much peer group tutoring and sharing also happen during a discussion, which can be teacher initiated or student initiated. This can be one-to-one, teacher and child or child and child, or one-to-many.

ROAD SAFETY

Roads and crossings around the school are often causes of concern to children. Encourage them to identify clearly what their worries are and to collect information that might support their request to a local authority for action to be taken.

Watching some children working on a self-initiated road safety project, the teacher noticed that they were losing track of their counting and getting very frustrated,

Teacher: 'What are you trying to do?'

Jane: 'We're finding out about...'

Quoc: 'About how many cars cross the crossing in five minutes.'

The teacher then asked,

'What's your problem then?'

The children explained their difficulty,

Quoc: 'We don't get the same number each time.'

Jane: 'We get muddled...er...especially when cars are going both ways fast.'

Teacher: 'What could you do about that, do you think?'

Darryl: 'We could...split up...like I'll do the ones going one way...'

Quoc: 'Yeah, and we'll do the ones going the other way.'

Teacher: 'Will you be able to count fast enough then?'

Jane: 'It's when there's a noise...you forget...get muddled up.'

Darryl: 'Yeah.'

Teacher: 'A tally might help. Do you know what a tally is?'

Five minutes later the children were quite confidently tallying. Later that morning, during a discussion with the rest of the class, these same children published the findings of their survey and showed the rest of the class how to make and interpret a tally. This type of situation, where a skill is taught when it is needed, used immediately and later explained to others as it is used to support a report, results in learning that is functional and can be transferred to other contexts.

HOW MANY MORE...?

Encourage the children to explore counting on as a strategy for subtraction questions.

Children can initiate or sign up for a discussion if they have a need or a problem. As a Year 3 class was working on a 'How many more...?' activity, several children having difficulty finding answers requested help. Keeping her questions fairly open, the teacher was able to build on what the children already knew and help them use strategies they already possessed.

Teacher: 'How are you trying to find out how many more you'll need?'

Jason: 'Take away.'

Katie: 'Doing sums.'

Teacher: 'When you go shopping how do you know how much change you'll need?'

Jason: 'They count the change into your hand.'

Suzie: 'Just give it to you.'

Katie: 'They go fifteen, and five is twenty.'

Teacher: 'How could counting on like that help you?'

Simon: 'Like if it's 21 you go 21, 22, 23, 24...50.'

Teacher: 'How would you know how many you'd counted on?'

Jason: I know...I know...you'd go, 21 and nine, that's 30...er...so you need two more tens to get to 50. That's 29.'

Katie: 'If you make it up to the next ten you know how many more tens you'll need. Tens is easy.'

A discussion also often results in the sharing of skills or strategies and often one child having difficulty will be helped by listening and watching others as they explain and demonstrate their strategy.

20 CENTS

What different ways can you find of making 20 cents?

David: 'I had to find out how many different ways I could make 20 cents. I thought there'd be 20, but there's lots. When I started I just wrote down any examples...but then Miss asked me how I'd know if I'd found them all...so I crossed that out and started again. First I did the obvious ones, 20, two tens, four fives, ten, twos and 20 ones. Then I did one ten with ten ones, and one ten with five twos and two fives. Then one ten, one five, two twos and one one...and like that...see? (holding up his paper).

Vikki: 'I never thought of doing it that way. I started with twenty ones and traded one at a time for twos, fives, tens. I don't think I got as many as you did.'

Children like to show their work and talk about it when it is complete: they want an audience. They gain in confidence by having their work valued by others. Also, children can be stimulated and challenged in response to a piece of published work. As the children show their work — drawing, model, chart or diagram — encourage them to report not just on their product but also on the stages of thinking, rethinking, problems and solutions that they encounterd on the way. Encourage them to ask each other questions during a discussion, and to make sensible comments. After a discussion, allow time for the children to respond to what has happened. They may need a minute or two to try the problem John's way, to test a hypothesis, to prove an answer to themselves, and to generate their own questions, problems or future actions based on what has been shown or said.

4

CHILDREN LEARNING FROM REFLECTING

Knowing what you know   Knowing how you know it

'You'll learn from your mistakes' is an expression we remember with distaste from childhood. We're not sure we ever knew what the mistake was or what we were meant to learn from it. We know now, of course, what we were meant to know then, that it is useful in a number of ways to reflect on:

- what we have been doing or learning;
- what we know now that we didn't know before, and
- what we would do differently next time.

The importance of this reflection process on the job and at the end of the job is vital in the maths lesson too, because the reflection process leads to two outcomes:

- knowing what you know;
- knowing how you know it.

Children usually find it straightforward to report on their activity in a verbatim fashion,

'First we did...then we did...etc.'

but to be really powerful, reflection needs to help children focus not so much on their action as on its implication. It is important, therefore, to encourage children to make generalisations from what they do and to express their understanding in terms that help them to know about what they know. The next stage is to contextualise the generalisation in terms of the activity that has just been carried out, and in terms of other situations to which the generalisation might apply.

KNOWING WHAT YOU KNOW

MISS MUFFET

Roll a die for Miss Muffet and move up or down a number line by that amount. The spider can move two in either direction. Miss Muffet is trying to get home before the spider catches her.

Six-year-olds Darryl and Sonya had played Miss Muffet on their own for some time before we were able to talk to them about how they were getting on. Sonya explained the method of counting that they were using for Miss Muffet.

> Sonya: 'When we get a number on the die we count it on our fingers.'
>
> Teacher: 'Why do you do that?'
>
> Sonya: Because on the board the numbers come out wrong...three and three is five. Because...if you're on six...and you get a three...you go six, seven, eight, and you put your counter on eight.'
>
> Teacher: 'Is that what you do, Darryl?'
>
> Darryl: 'I go...one, two, three, four, five, six...seven, eight, nine.'
>
> Sonya: 'Why do you count to six?'
>
> Darryl: 'Cause six is how many I'm on.'
>
> Sonya: 'Yeah, but you know you're on six, so you just go six seven, eight, nine...right?'
>
> Darryl: 'Oh!'
>
> Sonya: 'Try it...let's play again, okay?'
>
> Darryl: 'Yes.'

Hearing Darryl and Sonya reflect on their game, it's interesting to hear them talk about what they know. They know that three plus three is six; they know that counting on their fingers gives them the results they expect; Sonya knows that she does not need to count from one each time. As Sonya and Darryl reflect in this way Sonya realises that she knows something special and wants to share it with Darryl. Having expressed her simple strategy for counting on and having tried to explain to Darryl why it is a more efficient strategy than his, will have clarified and consolidated what she knows.

And what of their use of the number line? The teacher will come back to this or a similar game some other time when the time is right. Now, the time is right for learning, using Sonya's strategy.

REALISING YOU DON'T KNOW WHAT YOU THINK YOU KNOW

Occasionally being given the opportunity to show what you know results in the realisation that you do not really know it. This is what happened when a Year 6 class was invited to try this activity.

MAKE A MATHS DICTIONARY

Encourage the children to list and define the mathematical terms they think a junior class might need to know.

Our class chose to make a dictionary for a Year 4 class, and discussed which mathematical terms they found hard and which they found easy. Each child then chose a word that they felt confident with and able to define and/or illustrate.

LINE & LINESEGMENTS

There are 5 types of lines
There horizontal, vertical,
oblique, line segments and
parrallel. Parrallel lines can
go horizontal, oblique and
vertical but they have to be
the same length. horizontal
lines go straight across
vertical go straight up and
down oblique on an angle
          Line segments can
horizontal   go any way
          but g ot two little

parallel lines

Line segment

vertical →

oblique   Lines on
            the end
            of both sides

Multiplication 0

Multiplication is when you times a number for instants 2×3=6 or 2 lots of 3 =6 an eg

3 bunnies 2 × 3

and

3 little Bunnies

equals 6

= 6 lollies

Parallel Lines.

Parallel Lines:- are straight lines that will never meet no matter how far they go

For example:- train tracks never meet

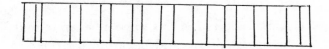

This is what they look like:-

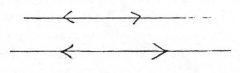

Parentheses.

– same as brackets. When part of
a problem is in Parentheses you
do that part first.

eg:– $60 + \overset{\text{Parentheses(Brackets)}}{(50+8)} \times 2 = \square$

Pronunciation:– (Par-ren-the-sēez)

Some children (see the examples above) were able to demonstrate what they knew by defining, illustrating and giving an example for their term. For others, though, there were surprises. Having chosen their terms, they found it very difficult to find words to express themselves or found that they could not exactly define the term. Examples of the term in action were relied on to convey the message. Addition is a case in point. Mark knew that he had to make his point clear to an audience and so gave examples to show what happened when numbers were added (see opposite). His approach though was rambling, he tried and tried again to define 'plus' but could not. He turned to the children near him who read his example and also had to struggle to find a way of describing addition. His teacher asked him to reflect on how he had learned addition when he was younger. He collected some MAB blocks and made up simple number sentences. Eventually he said out loud,

'A group with three in and a group with four in, now put them together...there's seven altogether.'

As he reflected in this way he began to make links to situations where he uses addition and began to list these to his friend.

'Money — 5 cents and 5 cents is 10 cents.'

The reflection process initially indicated to Mark that his understanding of addition was less developed than he thought. By further reflection, however, he was able to construct a much clearer understanding of addition and was able to define it verbally.

ADDITION

ADDITION means plus,add, and putting

together. ADDITION is a very easy sum

like if you get a two sents and a one sent, you can

Plus them and it will make 3 sente thats how easy

it is, and if you have some money you count it

and you are plusing that mean adding like if you

have a som like 10+5=15 and if the som has a

ten in it and a five you just have to look at

the ten and add the sum and then you will have

fiveteen and if you have a sum what the teacher

gives you jast add it

$$\begin{array}{r} \$1.00 \\ +\ 5 \\ 10 \\ \hline \$1.15 \end{array}$$

In Chapters 1 and 3 we described the progress of a class involved in investigating a 'Healthy Diet'. A highlight of that project was the children's understanding of notation used for quantities. As a consolidation of this, the class made notes in their journals about other contexts where this kind of notation is used. Here we had a simple example of the children confirming what they had learnt in the course of a project, not only in terms of the project outcome. Again, this was an opportunity for the children to reflect on 'knowing what you know'.

KNOWING HOW YOU KNOW IT

A group of children working on the 'Spider and Fly' (see page 14) felt they had explored the problem to its limit.

THE SPIDER AND THE FLY

The spider is trying to catch the fly. The spider and the fly move in turn from one junction to another. The spider moves first.

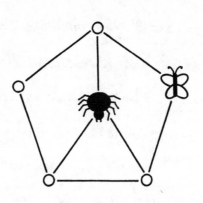

The children were asked to write in their journals about what they had done. Debbie had written,

The spider must stay at least 2 moves away from the fly to catch it (see fig. 1.4) The closer the spider gets to the fly, the more difficult it is to catch it.

Fig. 1.4

If the fly stays this far away from the spider it will take longer to be caught. If the spider stays 2 moves from the fly he will catch it quicker

Teacher: 'That's a good description of how to solve the problem. But how did you find that out? Try to think about what you did. It's as important to do that as it is to write about what you found out.'

The subsequent list of events that Debbie described included:

- playing the game with fingers instead of counters (just to see what happened);
- marking the moves on a diagram (very confusing when you have marked 24 moves);
- inventing another way of showing the moves (labelling the diagram and listing the labels moved to).

Debbie was then asked what was the most important thing in helping her to solve the problem. She replied,

'It was when we did the labels and wrote down the moves. It was easy then to see the spider kept on going to the same place.'

Debbie's strategy seemed a good one to share with the rest of the class,

'When everyone's had a go at the problem, maybe you could share that with them.'

Debbie wouldn't have been expected to see immediately the importance of drawing a diagram and inventing a suitable notation, but in her reflection on the process she had certainly pinpointed a key stage. At the report back session we found that others had the same difficulty. Though the class had invented a variety of methods, the reflection process helped us to establish that 'drawing a diagram' is often a key stage in solving a problem. To help the children remember the occasion, they were asked to write about what they felt they had learned in their journals, and if possible, to give examples of where 'drawing a diagram' helps.

The range of ideas that they wrote about gave the strong feeling that not only did they know (that 'drawing a diagram' is a useful strategy), but that they could contextualise this understanding and see its value in a variety of situations. To complete the session we had a brief period where the children shared their journals with others, something that gave them an even fuller understanding of the diagramming strategy.

NEW PROBLEMS FROM OLD

Looking back at the brainstorming session we had when we had written a large number nine on the board (page 18), and the variety of ideas that came from the children, we wondered whether we would ever be able to find a common thread for them to reflect on. As luck would have it, we were in for a surprise. This came about because, at our report back stage, two groups had been methodical in the way they had written out the facts that they had found out.

$$9 \times 1 = 9$$
$$9 \times 2 = 18 \qquad 1 + 8 = 9$$
$$9 \times 3 = 27 \qquad 2 + 7 = 9$$
$$9 \times 4 = 36 \qquad 3 + 6 = 9$$
$$9 \times 5 = 45 \qquad 4 + 5 = 9$$
$$9 \times 6 = 54 \qquad 5 + 4 = 9$$
$$9 \times 7 = 63 \qquad 6 + 3 = 9$$
$$9 \times 8 = 72 \qquad 7 + 2 = 9$$
$$9 \times 9 = 81 \qquad 8 + 1 = 9$$

Placing the children's work side-by-side we asked them to describe what they had done,

Multiplication group: 'We used a calculator!'

Addition group: 'We wrote out all the add sums you can do to get 9. And we didn't need a calculator. We knew the answers.'

Our efforts in putting the work side-by-side were soon rewarded by the multiplication group,

'They've got the same numbers as we have, but they were adding.'

Soon the whole class was involved in discovering that the digits of multiples of nine added to nine. The scene was set for further investigation, namely multiples of nine above 100, and a calculator was used by everyone. At the end of the double lesson the whole class had seen the value of reflecting on what you have done. Alice said,

'There's no end to the things you can find out.'

AIDS TO REFLECTION

To make sure that the reflection process is not haphazard, there are a few activities that we have found particularly valuable:

- **Demon lists**   The children make their own lists of number facts, tables or vocabulary to memorise. Whenever possible, the demon list should grow out of an activity that the children have been involved in and should match their interests.
- **Journal writing**   Impromptu reflections and ideas can be recorded in a journal in which the children make regular entries in an informal style, using words, symbols and illustrations that they feel are appropriate.

- **Personal dictionaries**   Using an alphabetically indexed book, the children write their own definitions of mathematical terms and describe strategies they have used. The dictionary should evolve as the children's understanding develops.
- **Report writing**   A carefully constructed report, either by a group or by an individual, gives the children the chance to enjoy revisiting work they have done earlier and to reflect on how well they now understand the reported topic.

These are concrete ways of encouraging the reflection process and, as such, will go a long way towards ensuring that standards are being maintained (or exceeded). Equally important, however, is the teacher's role in the process. Careful management of group and whole class discussion is needed to ensure that reflection is both educationally rewarding and socially enjoyable.

PART TWO

CLASSROOM APPROACHES

- ♦ Introduction
- ♦ Purposes for Using Mathematics
- ♦ Conditions for Learning Mathematics
- ♦ Shared Experiences for Learning Mathematics
- ♦ Assessment

INTRODUCTION

For some time researchers have observed infants as they strive to learn their first language. What is it that makes it possible for children to learn such a complex system so readily, and what are the implications of this for teachers? Basically, as language learners, children are exposed to language in all its richness and in a wide range of contexts. Children are, for a lot of the time, in the driver's seat, deciding when to talk, what to talk about and, in exchange, receiving praise, support and response. By valuing the infant's attempts, further contexts for real communication arise. This most vital ability to talk and communicate is not taught, rather it is learned in situ. Nor is it broken down into manageable and sequential units that can be digested and remembered and stored until required, or until enough piecemeal information is retained to build up a whole.

Learning in the language arts lessons now very much reflects this language acquisition model. Process writing puts the children in the driver's seat by inviting them to decide what to write about, which register or genre to write in, who to communicate with. Also, skills such as spelling and punctuation are accepted as having a developmental sequence. Early attempts at writing are not seen as incorrect, but rather as approximations that develop naturally into closer and finally 'correct' spelling and punctuation. Just as children naturally move from approximations and generalisations to the conventional adult form, so children can make these moves in writing and, we believe, in mathematics too.

Michael Halliday and Joan Tough have both researched the purposes for which children use language. The implications of these researches are beginning to affect classroom practice in the area of language arts. Teachers are now aware of the need to provide children with a wide range of contexts in which they hear, read, speak and write in a variety of modes — poetic, informal, hesitant, formal — and for a wide variety of purposes — to explain, to accompany or initiate action, to express feelings and moods. Again, we do not intend to list the purposes highlighted by Halliday or Tough. Rather we have taken those purposes and used them as a basis for investigating which purposes and genres (styles) are most commonly used in mathematics. The purposes and genres that we have identified are introduced and discussed in Chapter 5.

Brian Cambourne highlighted seven conditions under which children learn to talk. These include immersion, demonstration, expectation, responsibility, approximation, employment and feedback. In Chapter 6, these terms will be used to illustrate how the conditions are equally important to the learning of mathematics.

The 'shared book approach' described by Don Holdaway, in *The Foundations of Literacy* is now common practice in many classrooms. In essence, it is a sharing time that has all the cosy features of the bedtime story. In this environment the children learn, in context, about books: what they are, how they are organised, the conventions of print, as well as developing reading skills and strategies. Books written by the children themselves and class produced books are also used as 'shared books', providing purpose and confidence for the children.

This same type of 'shared experience' can, and we believe should, be a part of the maths lesson to foster a positive attitude to maths, confidence in mathematical ability, and, very importantly, a quiet, relaxed time where mathematics is the focus and incidental learning can occur. Chapter 7 covers this topic.

Lastly, in Chapter 8, we look at the question of accountability, in terms of both assessing children's progress in the maths classroom and involving parents in the educational process.

In summary, Part Two of this book is about utilising the many exciting trends in the language arts as inspiration for providing the kind of environment or learning experiences that will, we hope, provide the foundations for all children to see themselves not just as real writers, but also as real mathematicians.

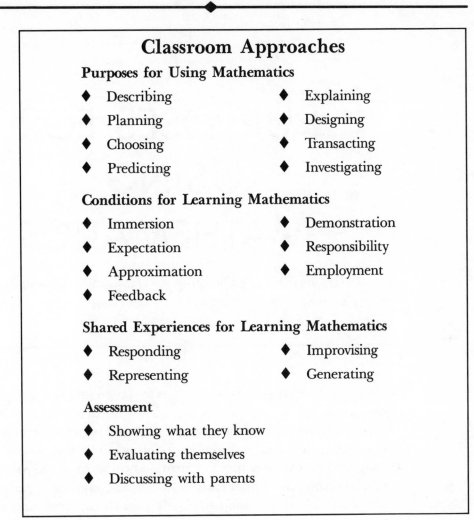

Classroom Approaches

Purposes for Using Mathematics

- Describing
- Planning
- Choosing
- Predicting

- Explaining
- Designing
- Transacting
- Investigating

Conditions for Learning Mathematics

- Immersion
- Expectation
- Approximation
- Feedback

- Demonstration
- Responsibility
- Employment

Shared Experiences for Learning Mathematics

- Responding
- Representing

- Improvising
- Generating

Assessment

- Showing what they know
- Evaluating themselves
- Discussing with parents

♦

5

PURPOSES FOR USING MATHEMATICS

Describing   Explaining   Planning   Designing
Choosing   Transacting   Predicting   Investigating

♦

As a result of recent research, many language arts guidelines now emphasise the importance of providing children with a wide range of contexts in which they can use and receive language in its four modes (speaking, listening, writing and reading). The suggestion is that the range of contexts will include formal and informal purposes and that children will have opportunities to use language for a variety of such purposes. These include using language to explain, report, predict, project, imagine etc. (see also Tough and Halliday). Also stressed in the guidelines is the importance of talking and writing to clarify thinking, share or extend ideas, and to reflect on ideas and activities.

No doubt these purposes for using language apply across the curriculum and as much to mathematics lessons as elsewhere. The question in our minds, though, is, 'Are there specific purposes for using mathematics?'

Our many observations of children and collections of children's work suggest that there are indeed particular purposes for using mathematics. Observations of children outside the classroom or school environment also suggest that children use mathematics spontaneously in these contexts too. We have identified eight different purposes for which children use maths. These are:

- describing
- explaining
- planning
- designing
- choosing
- transacting
- predicting
- investigating

This list can be a starting point for thinking about how to plan maths lessons and contexts that offer children the opportunity to use mathematics for as many purposes as possible. Also these purposes provide the basis for classroom observation and evaluation of the lesson content.

In what follows, we discuss the identified purposes in terms of appropriate language, to highlight the importance of getting children to talk about what they are doing and thinking. Through mathematical language comes an appreciation and understanding of mathematical concepts.

DESCRIBING

Children of all ages can be observed using mathematical language, concepts and techniques to describe the properties of objects, situations and places. They compare and describe properties in terms of size, shape, quantity, order, distance, speed, position and direction quite freely and spontaneously. Pre-school children describe and compare objects as part of their play,

'Look at our cubby house. Baby has the small pillow and the...the little chair. Daddy has the big one. He's tall.'

'We raced our cars. Mine's fastest...fastest...not big though. Mine's smallest. Look.' (directly comparing the two cars side-by-side)

These descriptions of characteristics, sameness and difference accompany action by young children. As they get older, descriptions of properties become more precise and depend less on the presence of the object or situation to be described or compared (i.e. they become more abstract), for example,

'We put these two beans into water on the same day. One's 14 centimetres high and it has got two big leaves and two new ones just breaking through. This one's 18 centimetres high. It's got two large leaves at the bottom of the stem, then at an angle to that and 5 centimetres above there are two more large leaves with three or four more bursting out at the tip...'

Children of all ages are also fascinated by changes. They describe changes in terms of lists, comparisons and cause/effect relationships, for example,

'My pattern is 2 squares, 1 triangle, 2 circles; 2 squares, 1 triangle, 2 circles. So it's like yours, 2 short, 1 middle, 2 long; 2 short, 1 middle, 2 long.

Describing is characterised by language concerned with identifying the properties of objects, comparisons of objects, relationships between objects, how things change and spatial relationships.

EXPLAINING

We have observed children of all ages explaining mathematical ideas and concepts. Often the explanations were for themselves, to clarify thinking or action. For example, four-year-old Cameron while drawing his trip to the koala sanctuary explained to himself where to place his kangaroos,

> 'There were two big ones... one big one here... where shall I put this one... a long way away. Two joeys... they've got to go in the middle... so... so... they can be looked after.'

Here Cameron was organising his thoughts, out loud, as young children often do to direct their actions.

Most explanations from older children were used to inform, clarify or persuade others of something,

> 'We got in a muddle when we were turning the triangle over so we marked each side with notches — one, two, three. If you do that, it's easy to see which side you are flipping over.'

> 'People wanted lots of different things to eat at the Christmas party. Well we couldn't have everything, so we chose the best things and we all did our survey. When we looked at the survey we decided to have...'

> 'No silly — you don't do it like that. Put your carry here — then you won't forget to add it in.'

> 'We thought that the tallest container would hold most. So we filled the jug and poured all the water in. It didn't fill the container. So we had to fill the jug again and pour some more water in. It's full now.'

What distinguishes an explanation from a description is frequently the structure of the language used. In the above examples, the key words that suggest explanation are the connectives, such as 'so' ('therefore'), 'if', 'when', 'then', which imply an argument rather than a description. The work of Collis and Biggs, *SOLO: A Taxonomy of Learned Outcomes*, provides valuable insights into children's abilities to structure outcomes, explanations being further along the scale of the taxonomy than descriptions. Children use the language of mathematics in explanations when they want to:

- use mathematical facts or statistics to put a point of view across or to justify an arrangement;
- devise oral or written instructions for making and constructing;

- give explanations of methods, approaches, techniques or strategies used to solve problems or find answers;
- provide explanations or 'proof'.

PLANNING

Children are not often observed using mathematics as a planning tool in school, although it is something they do frequently out of school.

'Let's go to the beach first. It won't be so hot if we do.'

'If you pay me to do the dishes all this week, I'll nearly have enough for Dream World.'

Given the opportunity, children can become quite adept at planning. From simple plans of what they will do in the next lesson to more complex arrangements needed for a successful class outing, children can readily assume responsibility for organising a series of events, particularly if we allow them to do this in relevant contexts.

The key to a good plan is the initial brainstorming session where a free flow of ideas is necessary before suggestions are censored. From a freely generated list of ideas comes a more mathematical stage of grouping and pruning as the important aspects of the plan emerge. This, in turn, can lead to an organised list of questions to ask or to a sequencing of events (by time), at which stage the plan is ready to be put into action.

Other features of planning are:

- *Identifying constraints*, e.g. time limits, spatial and financial constraints.
- *Ordering*, e.g. what should be done first/last?
- *Quantifying*, e.g. how many need to be catered for? How many sandwiches will we need?
- *Costing*, e.g. what is the bus fare?

Children planning the next day's timetable were observed ordering events and identifying constraints,

'If we do our writing first the fast ones can get on to their maths when they want to. 'It's best to do PE last — then you don't have to work when you're all hot and sticky.'

Characteristically, the language that children use in this kind of planning activity is concerned with time and sequence. Indeed planning, as an activity, provides opportunities for the children to think about time in real contexts and to gain an appreciation of the span of different time periods. Opportunities for costing and quantifying arise when children plan an outing to a favourite place, and activities like these often depend on calculators being available, as in the example below.

19.20	Ballarat to Melbourne
86.40	3 adults at $6.40
	27 children at $3.20
2.70	Boat trip on the Yarra.
13.37	3 adults at $1.00 ⎤ 10% discount
	27 children at $.55 ⎦ for a party
	Museum Free
	Art Gallery Free
9.90	Insurance 9.90
3.30	Train 3 adults at $ 1.10
	27 children at $ .30¢
8.10	
142.97	All together $ 5.30 each

When the plans are put into action, children have the additional bonus of seeing how mathematics helps them do things that they really care about.

DESIGNING

From their very earliest days, children are creative designers. Whether playing with blocks to make a tower that won't topple, or joining Duplo bricks to make a truck for teddy to ride in, they have a goal to reach and a design problem to solve. Problems such as how the pieces fit/join together and which materials or shapes will best suit the job, are aspects that children have to consider,

'I'm going to use these boxes and tubes for my robot. I think I can join them to make it bigger than me.'

In the primary years, designing offers children opportunities to use many aspects of number, space and measurement in an integrated way. Questions of appropriate size, proportion, ratio, pattern and order often arise,

'Would it help if I put the bed up high, with a ladder?'

'How much bigger do the back wheels need to be?'

'How much bigger than Jack does the giant puppet need to be?'

'Which pulley wheel would be best for this lifter?

Terms that define comparisons, cause/effect relationships and problem/solution relationships are characteristic of the mathematical language used when designing.

CHOOSING

Choosing, and deciding, are very common purposes for which children use mathematical ideas. For example, at the primary level choosing/deciding who goes first/last, the tastiest sweet, what to wear, what to play, or who to have for class monitor and voting on issues discussed in class, occurs frequently.

Children in the early stages of moral development (see Piaget or Durkheim) have a real need for fairness. They see things in terms of black and white and want 'right' answers to questions such as, 'Who goes first?'. We have seen children using 'dipping' rhymes (one potato, two potatoes), choosing the short straw, tossing a coin, taking votes and using simple statistics in an attempt to make decisions that are 'fair'.

In classrooms we have seen children conduct popularity polls to find the favourite television programme, star or sports personality. We have seen children design questionnaires and conduct surveys to answer questions such as,

'Should we have to wear school uniforms?'

'Do you think that these crossroads should have a pedestrian crossing?'

'Would you like after-school clubs?'

Children are also quite responsible consumers and can give an informal recommendation about 'best buys' at the school tuckshop, sweetshop, toyshop etc. In classrooms we have seen children using mathematics and statistics to make informed decisions about best buys, best routes and best places for a class outing. Children use cost, measurement, quantity and design tests for strength, durability, flavour, amount of lather etc. to make recommendations for informed choices and decisions.

TRANSACTING

Transacting is, we feel, the most common use of mathematics in the real world of both children and adults, yet it is probably the most neglected in school. Shopping, banking, trading etc. involve adults in transactions that use mathematical language and constructs. For children too this is the case. As they barter and trade with friends, shop, negotiate rules etc., children are necessarily transacting. It is in transacting that pencil and paper algorithms are the least effective. Children transacting in the real world use their own invented strategies or what Cockcroft (1982) refers to as 'folk methods'. Where in school do we facilitate and encourage the invention and use of folk methods in maths? In particular, how can we ensure that children who are confident with the methods they use in the real world, develop the same confidence in school? The following incident brought home to us how important this is.

One Saturday, as there was nothing in the fridge that could count as breakfast, we went down to the local convenience store. That's where we saw the grapefruit. At 16 cents each, here were just the thing. We picked out three plump ones and took them to the till. Serving behind the counter was Gary, a member of the Year 10 remedial maths set. We were wondering how he would make the calculation of 3 × 16 when we heard him mutter,

'Two add six makes eight.'

Then he said, full of confidence,

'Forty-eight cents, please.'

Why, we pondered, did he need to add six to two, and why did he look so unusually confident in his calculation? The assumption we made was that he didn't know the answer to 3 × 16 directly and wasn't confident to go through the long multiplication in his head. Had he done so, then we would have expected to have heard him mutter some, if not all, of the following:

Three sixes are eighteen.
Put down the eight and carry one.
Three ones are three.
Add one makes four.
That's forty-eight.

No, that was not his approach. Perhaps then what he had done was to break down the sum into parts that he could manage with confidence.

Three sixteens, can't do.
Try two sixteens.
Yes, that's thirty-two.
What's left? Sixteen.
I can add the ten, that makes forty-two.
Now the six. Two add six makes eight.
Forty-eight cents please.

The other purposes in our list cover activities that can be carried out individually, although many are best undertaken collaboratively. However transacting explicitly involves children in sharing ideas and questions, and negotiating with others. To help lift maths off the life-less page of the textbook, situations in which children experience mathematics as something alive and active need to be allowed for. Providing opportunities for transacting gives just this experience. If we look at the kind of language that is used in transactions, we often find that mathematical ideas are expressed in natural, informal lan-guage. Also typical of transactional situations is the use of mental arith-metic, often done in a way that suits the thinker and the problem, e.g. the strategy most commonly used for subtraction is counting on and estimates are made after rounding off.

In Chapter 2, 'Young Mathematicians at Work', all the examples provided were of children working collaboratively. As a technique for encouraging meaningful transactions, collaborative group work is para-mount. This is where the children trade ideas and suggestions in ways that are real for them. Also important are situations where mathe-matical ideas/concepts form the basis of the transaction that is taking place, shopping being the obvious example.

PREDICTING

This is something that children and adults do almost automatically. Predicting how many or how much of something is needed, predicting how much more will be needed; predicting what will happen if . . . I put another one on top . . . if . . . I take this one away when building or stacking objects; predicting changes that will occur by moving objects (e.g. furniture in a room . . . will it fit/suit?), combining items to make mixtures, or arrangements. For example young children doing junk modelling seem to sort the junk until they decide what to make and then will collect several boxes and begin work. Usually the boxes and junk selected are suitable in size and shape to the object being con-structed. Predictions have been made (perhaps by direct comparison, previous experience, or visualising) about which size, shape and quan-tity of items will be needed. Early experiences of fitting, counting, matching, pouring, spatial activities, patterning, ordering and time passing, all combine and become interrelated, forming the basis for much more complex mathematical prediction.

In language teaching, a common practice to help comprehension is to ask children to predict what they think a passage will be about from the heading alone. This encourages the children to bring to the front of their minds everything they know about a topic, and so make it easier for them to recognise new ideas, vocabulary and connections of which they were previously unaware. This technique also has pay-offs in mathematics teaching.

If, before undertaking a calculation, the children predict an answer, they can bring what they know about a situation to the fore and assess the subsequent calculation in the light of what they think an answer ought to be. In particular, with the growing use of calculators in the classroom, prediction has an increasingly important role to play.

At a straightforward level, using 'Guess and Press' activities is a good way of getting children to consider carefully what is going on when they use a calculator. For example, when asked to predict the result of,

3 [−] [+] 2 [=]

most children predict an answer of 1, not realising that the effect of pressing [+] is to overwrite the [−]. At a more advanced level, the calculator provides great scope for prediction in the context of trial and error methods. Trial and error can be used both as a problem-solving method, and as a way of introducing children to new ideas. The course books *Calculators in the Primary School* and *Calculators in the Secondary School* make a number of suggestions in these areas.

A recurring feature of calculator activities, when organised for group and whole class work, is the potential they provide for children to use the language of prediction: 'about', 'roughly', 'approximately', 'close to', 'accurate'. Freed from the burden of calculation, the children seem able to talk about their predictions and calculations much more fully than otherwise, using such terms as they do so.

INVESTIGATING

Much of the mathematical activity described in Chapter 2 has investigating as its core. Whether finding information in books, from surveys, by experimentation (on paper or physically), or other means, the key to investigating is to be systematic. Indeed, being systematic is such a key process in maths that we need to make sure that all children spend time investigating as often as possible. Please, no more,

'Daryll — you've got all these numbers here. I can't understand them, can you?'

If we look at the kind of language that is associated with investigating, we have found that it varies greatly, from incomplete and hesitant,

'...this is one...no, it's the same as that...try one like this.'

to well organised and methodical,

'That's done, all the shapes with three. What happens when we try to fit four shapes together?'

However, a common feature of the language children use when investigating is that it tends to be informal.* As the children collect information during an investigation, they also tend to use informal methods of representation. Rough tables, lists, sketchy drawings and plans are typical of such work. As with language, the informality of their activity does not necessarily imply lack of competence. Perhaps you can remember the last time you personally collected information for one reason or another. Hastily constructed lists of figures are very much the order of the day if your purpose is investigation, rather than presentation.

IN CONCLUSION

Why do we feel it is important to isolate different purposes for using mathematics? To answer this, we need to look at the reasons why the corresponding taxonomy has proved useful in the language field. Success in reading depends on children seeing the purposes of reading, deriving pleasure and information from what they read. Success in writing depends on having a purpose and an audience for writing. Mathematics, we feel, depends on similar prerequisites. Children need to see the purpose for using maths for pleasure, to gain information and to make things happen. Purpose can provide the motivation to want to learn and use mathematics. Purpose can also ensure that children care about the results and outcomes of their mathematical activity.

---

*It is worth mentioning here the distinction between competence and performance. A Canadian research project into language teaching (this being a key topic for a nation that comes close to being bilingual) uncovered a marked distinction between children's competence with language, that is, the level that they could competently comprehend, and their actual performance with language, that is, the language they actually used in classroom transactions. The level of competence was found to be far greater than the level of performance. In the same way, children, when left to undertake mathematical investigations on their own, frequently appear to regress in their use of maths, choosing to do things in ways with which they feel thoroughly comfortable (performance level), rather than use skills that only recently were acquired (competence level). It is, we feel, this distinction between competence and performance that accounts for children using informal language while involved in an investigation.

6

CONDITIONS FOR LEARNING MATHEMATICS

Immersion   Demonstration   Expectation   Responsibility
Approximation   Employment   Feedback

'I'm older than you, Jojo, but you're taller than me. You must have grown faster than I did.'

This snatch of conversation was overheard as two four-year-old cousins were talking about this and that. Under no pressure to compare and contrast, not asked to find the answer to a question, these children were expressing their world in mathematical terms. As with the process of early language acquisition, so most children find their own way of discovering and explaining mathematical ideas and concepts, drawing from the conditions of their environment.

Brian Cambourne as a result of his own research introduces seven conditions or prerequisites which he believes make the learning of talking universally successful. The same headings apply equally well to the acquisition of mathematical ideas. In this chapter we take Cambourne's seven conditions and show how they apply to mathematics and how these conditions for learning can be fostered and continued in school.

IMMERSION

In their early years, children experience an environment that abounds with number, shape and measurement. They are surrounded by day-to-day activities that have a mathematical foundation, activities such as,

shopping: stacking shelves, trolleys, boxes; handing over money; signs with numbers; various shaped and sized containers
washing: sorting, filling the basket/machine; measuring the powder/rinse aid; matching pegs with garments as the washing is hung out

88

cooking: sorting, collecting, measuring, counting, emptying, filling, pouring etc.

Much of this flood of experience is articulated for children by those around them, but children also have the time and motivation to explore their environment for themselves. For example, children role play the actions of characters they see in real life and on television. Even playing in the yard, children spontaneously collect and sort pebbles, leaves and twigs, they pour from one container to another, arrange and rearrange piles of dirt or sand. Children also imitate counting, '4, 8, 4, 2' and look for shapes — 'want another round one' — as they have heard siblings or *Playschool* do. Manufactured toys are designed for children to sort, stack, order and match shapes and numbers to objects. In this way they are naturally immersed in mathematical input.

HOW DOES THIS RELATE TO THE CLASSROOM?

There is no need for this natural and spontaneous immersion in mathematics to cease or change in a school environment. We now know that for children to want to become readers and writers they need to see reading and writing as purposeful activities. Classrooms now reflect this by being places where children write and read labels, signs, messages, books, reports, class newspapers and much more too. They are immersed in written material.

In a similar way, we can immerse children in mathematics. We can display their mathematical models and reports. We can involve children in organisational aspects of the classroom — where things could fit, be stored, displayed, how many of a particular item are needed, how many children need pencils, how much money has been collected etc. — always sharing the results and methods to find answers with the children. If children are too young to work these things out for themselves, they can at least see you doing them and how you do them.

We can collect everyday objects that may stimulate mathematical thinking or investigation. For example, shells and buttons, if left out for young children to play with, will result in sorting, counting, matching and pattern activities. Children will experiment and invent their way towards number, space and measurement. Older children, too, if left with an assortment of odd-shaped boxes, will look to see how they were made, how they are joined, how they stack, what could fit inside. This is the same kind of play and exploration that they were immersed in as young children.

For older children, the media also provide mathematical contexts often neglected in schools. Statistics, figures, tables, graphs, plans and maps all feature largely in newspapers and can be brought into school.

The key point here is not that children pursue every available mathematical avenue, but that they are exposed to and immersed in whole and meaningful uses of mathematics — maths that they can respond to if they want, when they want, and in any way they want. Often children hear a word or phrase many times but do not use it; they may not feel confident to use it. This is the difference between language competence (what they know) and language performance (what they use). This same competence and performance gap exists in mathematics. The children rarely use their most recently acquired maths skill or concept, preferring to fall back on some old and trusted method. By immersing children in mathematics we broaden their mathematical bases.

DEMONSTRATION

A child's first encounters with mathematics are accompanied by repeated demonstrations in their own environment. For example, early experiences with counting may include rhymes, counting stairs, objects, number songs. Parents, singing 'Baa Baa Black Sheep' to their children, do not expect the counting to be echoed parrot fashion immediately. They sing these songs and count the steps out loud because they know that children enjoy these activities. Letting a young child help with the washing-up, measuring and pouring ingredients when you cook, having pouring toys in the sand or bath are simply experiences of measuring, of full and empty, and yet we repeat these experiences many times, not teaching directly, just demonstrating when and how these activities are appropriate. Somehow, as parents, we realise that children need this variety and repetition of experiences from which to develop concepts of number, space and measurement.

HOW DOES THIS RELATE TO THE CLASSROOM?

Time is a constant pressure at school. So too is the constraint of curriculum guidelines. Demonstration is a common feature of many classrooms, demonstration, for example, out of context, by the teacher, of how to do takeaways. Such demonstrations do not show how, when or why we do these takeaways in real life. Nor are they repeated frequently in many different ways; nor are children encouraged to ask questions, interpret and try their own ways.

Demonstration, to be useful, needs to take a much more varied approach. For example, a need for the skill or concept could arise and the children, using a variety of concrete objects, could try to solve the problem by themselves, demonstrating and describing to each other their approaches, successful and unsuccessful. You could invite the children to join you in deciding how to approach the situation. Together an algorithm or heuristic can be worked out, charted and displayed. The method used can then be tested in other similar contexts, the whole approach being related to:

- how the skill/concept is used in the real world;
- what method is appropriate to the real world;
- repetition and transfer of the skill or concept to other situations immediately.

EXPECTATION

Ironically, parents expect their children to become successful language users, but do not have similar expectations for their children to become successful mathematics users. In fact quite the reverse is often the case,

> 'I was no good at maths when I was at school...so I don't expect my children will be.'

is quite a common statement. Maths is seen to be hard, an attitude that can rub off onto children. Older siblings, too, perpetuate this expectation that maths is difficult.

HOW DOES THIS RELATE TO THE CLASSROOM?

It is Day One in school and the teacher asks her five-year-olds to write a story. The children respond with scribbles, scribbles with some letters mixed in, strings of letters or, in a few instances, some actual words. Not floored by this the teacher asks the children to read their stories, and they do. No one says to them, 'That's not writing' or 'This doesn't make sense'. The children are confident that they have written a story, that they can read it, and that it does make sense.

In Years 2 and 3 and beyond, this expectation of children as writers persists. Children invent spellings, they cross out, rearrange, start again, in the expectation that they will eventually write a polished piece.

We need to establish this kind of expectation of children as mathematicians too, not telling them that something is wrong or poorly executed, but allowing them the time, freedom and expectation that they will, in time, move to closer approximations of real mathematics, that they will master the mechanics, understand the concepts, work out their own algorithms and strategies with which to find answers. In short, all children will be mathematically competent.

RESPONSIBILITY

There is, as yet, no published curriculum for the pre-school years. Depending on what is happening around them, children are usually left to themselves to decide what to explore and engage with, and they appear to take responsibility for when they will master a particular shape puzzle, or what structures to make with their bricks. Children also decide when they have gone far enough with the activity.

HOW CAN CHILDREN TAKE RESPONSIBI-
LITY FOR THEIR LEARNING IN SCHOOL?

We have all experienced the rapid and exciting way children learn when
they are ready to. We have also experienced the stubborn, uninterest-
ed child who does not want to learn what we've planned, or who learns
almost by default.

By setting time aside for children to work on topics that interest them,
we can put children back into the position they managed so well as
pre-schoolers: that of taking responsibility for their own learning, choosing what to work on, how and how far to pursue it, and deciding when
it is complete. With young children this is made possible by controll-
ing the resources available. If a child has limited experience with length,
providing sticks, ribbons, strings and paper strips of varying lengths
is likely to result in some measurement activity. What that activity is,
however, will be determined by the child.

Older children can generate their own questions or respond to
problems posed by other children. Negotiation also becomes possible.
Children can be let into the secret of what skills should be mastered
this term and be given responsibility for choosing the order of attack.
They can also be allowed to develop these in their own way, deciding
themselves when they are ready to move on.

The key point here is that children take responsibility for their own
learning. They can seek help if and when they need it. They can decide on their own approach, using concrete objects until they decide
they do not need them any more, repeating an activity as often as they
need to. They can stop when they are satisfied, go at their own pace
and, above all, decide for themselves if and when they have been
successful.

By giving children responsibility for their learning we are allowing
them to initiate activity, to set their own goals and know when they
have achieved them, and also to have ownership of their work.

APPROXIMATION

As children begin to count, at first they approximate real counting,
1, 2, 5... They later approximate touch counting, saying 1, 2, 3, 4,
5 much more slowly than they are touching objects. Eventually one-
to-one correspondence results in the objects being accurately counted.
Mathematical language goes through similar stages of approximation.
Our twins knew what a circle was and insisted on calling all objects
with curved edges 'circles' for quite some time. They have also heard
a circle with a hole in it being called a donut on *Sesame Street*. They
now call anything round with a hole in it a donut, circles are donuts,
reels of masking tape are donuts. We are not anxious about this, we
know that they are working towards closer approximations of mathematical terms.

WHAT DOES THIS MEAN IN THE CLASSROOM?

The research into children learning to spell and write shows this move towards closer approximations to the real things as a normal developmental sequence. The stages that children go through on the road to correct spelling are now an accepted and expected part of learning to write.

In maths, too, there are many developmental stages on the road to accurate answers. We need to look at what children are doing, not at what they produce, if we want to see how they are thinking and what their current understandings are. For example, David was using his number line to work out answers to some questions he had set as a workcard for the Maths Interest Centre. He had set himself the job of providing an answer card. When his teacher looked at his answers they were all wrong. She asked David,

Teacher: 'What kind of questions have you set, hard or easy?'

David: 'Easy.'

Teacher: 'How are you working out the answers?'

David: 'On my number line.'

Teacher: 'Can you show me how you do it?'

David: 'I put my finger on the first number...er...eight, and then I count on, one, two, three, four, five, six, and look what number I've got to.'

Watching David's moving finger as he counted along revealed that he counted the one he was on before jumping to the next number.

Teacher: 'David, I don't get the same answer as you. I get fourteen. Look.'

David watched and then tried it himself; he still got thirteen and asked,

David: 'What do you get for this one?'

David realised that he was one out each time, but not why, and changed all his answers. Only then did he want to investigate why. He wanted to find a way of getting the right answers by himself now that he knew what the answers were.

On another occasion we watched a pair of children trying to measure the school corridor. They had several metre sticks which they laid out end-to-end. They did not have enough, so they went back to the classroom for more. There weren't any more there so they brought 40 centimetre rulers out with them. Now they had covered the length of the corridor but could not work out an answer. Back to the classroom for 30 centimetre rulers. Still no result. Then Claire said,

'My dad makes a mark when his tape runs out.'

as she began to pick up all the rulers and metre sticks. They set to marking and replacing just one metre stick and soon had a result. After at least two years of using objects, and mixed objects and the metre sticks, the children were beginning to approximate real measuring in standard units, and abstract ways. In their own time and their own way they were becoming competent measurers.

EMPLOYMENT

Before school, children are not restricted in the time they spend practising a skill nor in the uses to which they put their newfound skills. As we observed our own children learning to build towers with their blocks, we noticed that several extended periods every day were employed in trial and error building. This has gone on for months as they try to scale new heights with their towers. Bit by bit they have worked out which sizes and shapes to use first, exactly where to balance the next block. They are now proficient tower builders and yet they still return to their blocks frequently. They talk about the tower that goes 'high, high to the sky' and this is their own personal challenge every time they build.

WHAT ARE THE IMPLICATIONS OF THIS IN THE CLASSROOM?

There seem to be two main points here, one being that children need plenty of time to explore a medium or activity. Chopping time up into little segments, interrupting the flow of concentration is not conducive to exploration and learning. The other point is that children (and adults too) need a purpose for pursuing a topic or activity. There is a limit to how many times a child will pursue a topic when the only reward is extremely deferred gratification — 'some time in life you may need to...'! The twins had time and purpose and were meaningfully employed in their activity. They had something they wanted to do and a reason for wanting to do it. They were developing manipulative and spatial awareness skills that they could immediately transfer to other situations.

FEEDBACK

Feedback is self-explanatory. We all want to know how we are doing — now — not next week or after the test. We want praise, ideas, help, challenges now, while we are still involved, not tomorrow when the interest has waned. Young children demand this instant feedback and adults are not very different. Most of all we want constructive criticism.

7

SHARED EXPERIENCES FOR LEARNING MATHEMATICS

Responding   Improvising   Representing   Generating

Many primary classrooms now take a shared book approach to reading. This approach is based on the work of Don Holdaway, whose research looked into the background experiences of high progress readers. As a result of this work, classrooms began to foster aspects of being read to at home in the classroom. Key features of this approach are that books are shared in a relaxed and comfortable atmosphere, and children are invited to join in or respond freely to the books, learning skills in the context where they have real meaning. Big Books, with large print and clear pictures so that every child can see, are used for this purpose. In many infant and some junior classes too, Big Books are being used in all curriculum areas. Manufactured books and Big Books often provide stimulus for science or social studies (e.g. *Bonnie and Clyde* and *My Grandma Lived in Gooligulch*) as well as language arts lessons. In response to such books, research is undertaken and new Big Books written.

In this chapter we explore this shared book approach and how it works for maths too. Children's literature can provide many mathematical starting points and so too can rhymes and jingles, the children's own writing and television.

RESPONDING

Young children in particular respond spontaneously to stories and rhymes. Perhaps older children lose the motivation to respond freely and creatively to such stimuli because it is not normally considered valuable by teachers of older children. The types of responses that children make to stories and rhymes can be very varied. For example, we have noticed that in classrooms where shared book experiences and improvisations on stories and rhymes are a common part of the language arts programme, children spontaneously improvise on number rhymes. In one classroom the children were singing 'Five Little Ducks Went Swimming One Day' while seven children, one the mother duck, one the father, and five ducklings, dramatised the actions. After the rhyme the teacher asked,

'Shall we sing that again, but this time have a new family of ducks?'

The children agreed, but one little girl said,

'We can change it, change it. This time two little ducks get lost.'

The teacher agreed and the singing began again, this time with long pauses while the children counted how many were left and discussed what to do for the last verse since there weren't two ducklings left any more. The children began to ask why there was only one duck left, had they counted incorrectly? The rhyme was repeated, using fingers for ducks this time (the children's suggestion). No, they hadn't counted incorrectly. The children were puzzled by this and began to make suggestions for solutions. Finally one child stated quite excitedly,

'If they go off in twos then they'll have to come back in twos won't they?'

It was decided and a new family of seven was chosen, mum, dad and five ducks. The first two ducks were sent off, then the next two and surprise, surprise, there was only one left. Puzzlement again, until Sophie said,

'That's it...got it now...we need another one duck. There's got to be six little ducks.'

And using her fingers she demonstrated 'one, two..., three, four..., five, six.' Soon the rest of the children were counting in twos on their fingers too. The rhyme was successfully dramatised this time and then Jason asked,

'Suppose we lose three ducks each time, will we need five or six little ducks?'

Not the usual type of mathematical activity for five-year-olds, repeated addition, nor would we normally expect five-year-olds to be investigating their own questions. But with a teacher who really listens to her children, takes occasional risks and lets the children have responsibility for setting the pace, anything is possible.

Still with five-year-olds, but this time not number, but spatial awareness, we once watched a group of four five-year-olds making up their own story for *Changes, Changes* by Pat Hutchins. After the story they immediately ran and asked the teacher if they could build with the bricks. Hands on the bricks and without a word to each other, they simultaneously started to hunt for and match the actual bricks in their box to the ones needed for the first house. Occasionally a shape or size could not be found so discussion and constant reference to the illustration would result in a substitute being chosen. Only when the necessary bricks had been found and systematically set out flat (like the one in the book) did the children begin to build. As they did so little arguments developed, such as,

'No, you can't put that one there. It...it's got to go on the other, over here. They've got to be the same on both sides. Look!' (pointing at the picture)

So here we see five-year-olds being systematic, attending to size, matching 3-D shapes to the 2-D illustration, trying to attend to symmetry and balance, and at the same time working from a plan. Again the children were working at an unexpected level of sophistication, secure in the knowledge that they could initiate, sustain and have ownership of their own work.

IMPROVISING

On another occasion in the same classroom *Rosie's Walk* had been the shared book. The children had made up their own story for the pictures using positional terms they already knew and hearing some new ones from the teacher. Later that afternoon one group of children was desperate to play with the farm animals. The teacher wondered why the sudden interest and then discovered the children improvising on *Rosie's Walk* to make up other positional stories. These children were invited to demonstrate and tell these new stories to the rest of the class. Over the next day or two the sandpit was transformed into a farmyard and, at the children's request, labels, 'behind', 'next to', 'through', were made so that the children could make up a story, label the route, and then invite a friend to try to retrace it. The class teacher had not planned or directed this, it had come from the children in response to *Rosie's Walk*. The teacher was delighted, because for most of the children in her class English was a second language and earlier attempts to teach positional terms in traditional ways had been ineffective. Now the children were using those terms and other more sophisticated ones not anticipated by the teacher to reconstruct a physical picture map story in the sandpit. The context provided the motivation to develop and use exactly the term to describe each action.

Haydn

5 hairy, monsters
In a dungeon deep
3 of them had big teeth
And two of them are scarey

Rhymes like 'Ten Apples on a Tree' are easily improvised on by the children as shown in the picture above. Here the children have adapted the rhyme to contexts of interest to them, and have drawn pictures to show their own number stories that suit their current developmental level. The beauty of this type of activity is that all the children can work at their own level, using numbers they are already confident with to ensure success, or challenging themselves to go beyond what they can currently do. In this case, the class's new rhymes were made into a Big Book for shared book time. Such books are usually the most sought after for personal reading time. The children read and try out the number stories and problems presented. The 'Noah's Ark' rhyme, too, led to a class of seven-year-olds spontaneously using this as a challenge to learning their tables.

'Suppose the animals went in three by three/four by four, how many would go in?'

Each group handled this differently, counting on to find answers, setting out blocks in threes, fours etc. and drawing pictures. One group built up a graph for each table. At the end of two maths lessons each group presented its work and a report to the rest of the class. The group building up the graphs noticed that 4 × 3 and 3 × 4, 4 × 5 and

5 × 4 etc. gave the same results and soon worked out that there were not actually a large number of tables to learn — information gratefully received by the rest of the class.

REPRESENTING

Millions of Cats was responded to by a class of seven-year-olds in a way that involved the whole school,

> 'What's a million?' they asked.
> 'What would a million cats be like?'

At first the class suggested that they should all draw and paste cats onto their class display board. In every odd minute the children were drawing cats. They soon spilled out into the corridor but still there were less than 1000. At morning parade the help of the rest of the school was elicited. Soon cats were being drawn and pasted all over school. With cats emerging from everywhere the problem of counting them all became apparent. Older children were enlisted to help with this. Cats were ringed and grouped in 100s. Even then by the time 5000 were counted it was apparent to all that to count to a million, even in hundreds, would take a long time and also that it would take forever to draw one million cats. Despite this and the abandonment of the project, every child in the school had had a real experience of large numbers, and had come closer to understanding what a million of anything would be like.

Older children too like to respond to, improvise on and represent stories and rhymes. A group of 11-year-old children whose teacher had just read an extract from *Alice in Wonderland* became fascinated by how big things must have been to Alice after she had shrunk. In one part of the room an argument was underway,

> 'Just think, a table would have looked as big as a house.'

> 'Don't be silly, it wouldn't.'

> 'Would.'

> 'Prove it!'

> 'How?'

> 'Dunno.'

> 'I know, how big is a house? If we knew how big a house is we could find out how big it is to us.'

> 'Yeah...then we could find out how big a table is to Alice.'

This group of children began to devise ways of finding out how tall a house is and then were stuck. What they wanted was to express their relationship to a house as a ratio. They tried to explain to the teacher what they wanted to do and a skills session on ratio provided them with the technique they needed, when they needed it, but without taking away ownership. They were given a technique to use, not a solution to their problem.

Television also provides occasional contexts that cause children to want to respond mathematically. Once when two Year 1 classes were put into one room until a supply teacher arrived the class teacher switched on the tail end of *Sesame Street*, just in time for Count Von Count, counting sheep to help him sleep. *Sesame Street* over, the teacher, still waiting for aid, handed out paper and pencils so that the children could draw a picture,

Several children [groaning in unison]: 'What shall we draw?'

Teacher: 'Anything you like.'

Children: 'Can we draw a Count Von Count picture and see how many we can count?'

Teacher [relieved]: 'That sounds great.'

Practically every child present chose to do this and all around the room children were drawing pictures of things they would like to count. Counting and writing captions and labels were just one aspect of this activity. The sharing and discussion afterwards provided many more counting and number recognition opportunities. So pleased were the children with their results that a class book was made of the efforts and is still a class favourite.

On another occasion a class of children watched a programme in which the maze at Hampton Court was featured. This captured the imagination of most of the class who wanted to know more about the Hampton Court maze. They also wanted to make mazes and see if they could write down instructions for getting into the maze and then reverse them to get out. There were many growth points for the children here. The practicalities of designing mazes that were complex and yet did not cut off a way of getting to the middle proved quite taxing. Trying to make the longest path in the smallest maze possible was just one of the challenges that the children grappled with. Lunchtime maze making and breaking competitions sprouted up across the school, permission having been granted for the children to draw chalk mazes on the paved area. These had to be hosed down by two children every afternoon after school.

GENERATING

The range and number of books available in Big Book format is limited. Teachers have responded to this shortage by painstakingly making their own Big Books. In some classrooms the children too are involved in making Big Books. Where children have contributed to the making, writing and illustrating of Big Books, important aspects of learning and attitude are fostered. Perhaps most important is the sense of pride and achievement that children feel on completion of a published Big Book, the fact that the time, care, research and accurately and attractively presented work have paid off. Because children have used maths creatively, with a purpose, and have shared it with others they want to do more. This contributes to a positive attitude towards mathematics.

So how do children go about generating their own Big Books? The most common technique, as stated earlier, is that of improvising on a particular story or rhyme pattern. Take *The Very Hungry Caterpillar* for instance. The children can choose a different creature that starts life from an egg, such as a tadpole, bird, dinosaur or fish, and list what it eats day by day and then make up a suitable punchline.

Even simpler is to stick with the caterpillar as the children in the photograph on the previous page have and just change the food each day. As the children do this they are counting out a set number and reading and writing numerals, but in a meaningful and purposeful context. They will soon see how successful they have been when they share their individual or group books with others.

Inspired by a Paddington Bear Omnibus one class of eight-year-olds improvised on *Paddington Hits the Jackpot*. Some children changed just the maths questions and made up their own tricky answers, while others put themselves as the hero and changed the questions. In both cases the children worked really hard trying to think of questions that could have more than one answer. Examples ranged from,

MC: 'If you had five sweets to start with and I gave you five more, how many would you have?'

A : 'None.'

MC: 'Wrong.'

A : 'No... if I have sweets I always eat them all at once so I'd have none left.'

to

MC: 'If it takes you twenty steps to the corner, how many will it take you to go there and back?'

A : 'Thirty-two.'

MC: 'Wrong.'

A : 'No... I took long steps coming back because a bear was chasing me... so I couldn't tread on the cracks.'

For this last example the children worked really hard to come up with measurement questions and answers.

A Year 1 teacher asked a Year 5 colleague if her class would like to write some Big Books for her children. After some discussion it was decided that the Year 1 teacher should introduce this idea to the Year 5 class herself. She took along *A Pet for Mrs Arbuckle*, a class favourite, and read it to the children to give them some idea of the sort of story that goes down well with Year 1 children. She also talked to the children about what her Year 1 class was learning about at that time. She asked the children not to illustrate the stories because it would be exciting for the Year 1s to do that themselves. In response to this request many children spontaneously improvised on the Mrs Arbuckle story pattern. Two girls really mastered this and wrote a story called 'The

Perfect Bone', about a dog who dreams about his perfect bone, and seeing the door open, runs off to look for it. After a long adventure he comes home tired and hungry to find that his perfect bone has been waiting there for him all the time. As the dog searches for his bone he looks in a variety of places, *on* a bin, *under* some bushes, *behind* Bozo's kennel, but all the bones he finds are opposites and all have something wrong with them, *'too long'*, *'too short'*, *'too rough'*, *'too smooth'*. The emphasis on positional language and opposites was tailor made for the Year 1 children, at that time of the year. Each page of the book was discussed in the Year 1 classroom and the children took great pains to match their pictures to the text. The Year 5 girls had a tremendous feeling of pride and success and so too did the Year 1 children who illustrated the book. As a result of illustrating this book, the Year 1 class had a spate of drawing positional pictures and writing matching captions and stories. Often, little flaps were stuck onto a picture concealing a hidden object. Only after reading the story or caption could the flap be lifted to find the hidden object.

BIG BOOKS DON'T HAVE TO BE STORY BOOKS

So far, all the examples of stories to use provided in this chapter have been fictional. Literature has much to offer but other types of books can be shared equally successfully. Sometimes a fictional story or rhyme can be used to stimulate a research project and may then result in a factual Big Book. For example, in response to 'Rapunzel' one group of children began to question whether it was possible for anyone to have hair that long. An hour spent in the library reading the *Guinness Book of Records* and books about the body provided some interesting information and questions for further research. One such question was,

'If hair grows 1 centimetre a month, how long could our hair grow by our age?'

followed by,

'Does anyone in our class have hair that long?'

Other questions based on the *Guinness Book of Records* included,

'Who has the weakest/strongest hair in our class?'

'Who has the shortest/longest hair in our class?'

A factual book about hair, hair care, and hair records for the class resulted from this story, and the folktale *Quick Eye* had a similar effect, with the children wanting to find out how far they could see, stretch, throw and run. Again a class fact book was presented based on a week's very sophisticated measuring activities, most of which took place on the school oval. This type of activity totally involves the children; they generate questions, find ways of answering them, often using much more sophisticated techniques than we would ever expect, and experiment with different ways of showing and reporting their findings. They sustain this type of work because it is relevant and meaningful to them. Children are also very egocentric so have an additional interest in such topics, borrowing these books time and time again to revisit and re-explore their personal facts.

OTHER FORMS OF WRITING

Other books stem from having something to mathematise about. Ideas for these include the following.

EXPERIENCE BOOKS

Here the children do something and then illustrate and write about it. Year 1 children, for instance, could visit the local shops, taking a few photographs of shapes, displays, the shopping process and environmental print, collecting leaflets and advertising brochures. These and children's illustrations drawn afterwards can then be used to make a class Shopping Book.

Year 4 children might go on a tessellation hunt, photographing, copying or making rubbings of examples they find for a class tessellating book.

Year 6 children might conduct a survey into something topical or generally interesting, presenting their findings, representations and conclusions as a report in the Big Book format.

CONCEPT BOOKS

Here the children can take a topic that they are currently studying, for example, measurement co-ordinates, algebra etc., and brainstorm their current understandings and knowledge of that concept. Headings like 'What is Algebra?', 'When is Algebra Useful?', and 'Some Examples' can be included, and will each provide scope for a group to write and illustrate a chapter for a Class Book. As they work on their chapters the children will realise what they do and do not understand, will ask questions and advice, try out some examples, share and refine their ideas and strategies and possibly do some research. As a result their understandings will have deepened and broadened as they discuss and reflect on what they know and how they know it.

PERSONAL DICTIONARY

These have the same effect but on a smaller scale. At the Year 1 level class-made dictionaries can show just one word and an illustration plus examples (e.g. square). At a Year 6 level they can be much more detailed as shown in the following example.

PERPENDICULAR

① A perpendicular line is like a vertical line (straight) which goes up and down and touches 2 surfaces.

② A perpendicular line is not either oblique nor horizontal (bent) it is straigh up and down.

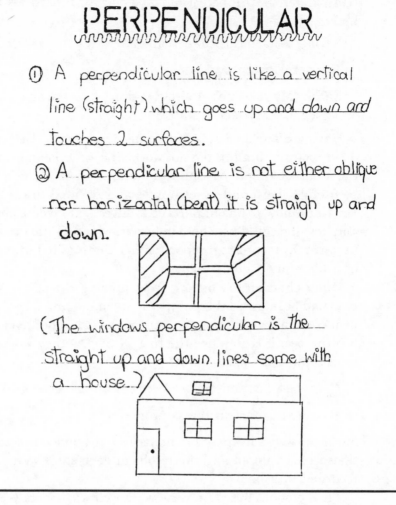

(The windows perpendicular is the straight up and down lines same with a house.)

PUZZLE BOOKS

There are many books around that present mathematical puzzles and riddles. These have a special appeal to children who usually work out the answer to the riddle and then enjoy hearing the trick answer. When children write their own riddles they are engaged in trying to design contexts for the riddles, in working out the real answer and also a nonsense answer.

THEME BOOKS

Theme books can arise when the children become interested in a particular aspect of mathematics and want to pursue it further. Shape is a recurring example with young children who enjoy using templates and inset trays to make pictures of, for example, houses, flowers, people, cars and animals. As children do this they begin to explore the properties of shapes and to relate shapes to their environment, refining their models or pictures as they do so. At the beginning of her shape picture, Karla made a man with a round head and round body. Later she rubbed it out and began using ovals for heads and bodies,

Karla: 'What's this shape called?'

Teacher: 'It's an oval.'

Karla: 'My face isn't a circle. I don't know anyone with a circle for a face. My face is an oval.'

Having discovered this interesting fact, Karla tried using ovals for other pictures, but this did not work. She went on an ovals hunt around the room looking at objects and pictures to see where else ovals would be useful. She found no examples and decided to try 'oblongs' next. For Karla now it was important to investigate where shapes occurred and how she could use them in her drawings. Quite naturally the need to research, record and report on her findings led to the construction of a book just called 'Shapes'.

Older children too benefit from making theme books. Two Year 6 boys had been asked if there was a way of making sure that their opponent could not win at noughts and crosses. The children looked at which was the best box to place the first 'X' in. As they worked they began to ask questions like,

'Can you play noughts and crosses on a bigger grid?'

'Would you start in the same place?'

For three weeks in spare moments and at home these and other questions were explored and the results at each stage were illustrated and recorded in a book.

Theme books based on verse work well with Years 1–3 children who can improvise on the rhymes, jingles and songs that abound to make up more of their own.

JOURNALS
Every child should be encouraged to keep a maths journal, a place where ideas, strategies, rough work and worked examples of problems can be recorded. The journal too is a place where children can record attitudinal aspects such as how they feel about a particular topic, what they do/do not understand and any problems they are having with a concept. Initially children find this difficult and do not know what to write in their journals.

Support at this early stage can take the form of questions to prompt thinking, for example,

'Was there anything you didn't understand in maths today?'

'What was a good/bad moment as you worked?'

'What method did you use to find answers?'

'What would you like extra help with?'

'What did you learn?'

'Is there an example you'd like to record in your book?'

As soon as possible though, children should take responsibility for their journals and what goes into them. A Year 5 teacher we worked with set aside five minutes at the end of each lesson for children to record anything they liked about the maths lesson. For the first two weeks the comments were at the level of,

'I liked this lesson.'

'I found this lesson hard.'

'I used doubles.'

The teacher found time to discuss journal entries with the children, asking what they found hard, what they liked etc. Slowly the children began to realise that their journal entries were respected and that the teacher wanted to use the journals as a way of knowing how to help them. Soon the children were writing things like,

'I knew how to do the divide bit and the adding bit but I don't know what an average is.'

'I couldn't get the right answer. I checked my working out on the calculator, it was the same as mine — but my answer is the wrong one. I don't know what I did wrong.'

The journal can fulfil several purposes as described earlier, and used at the end of the lesson is invaluable in the process of reflection. Reflection, however, does not just happen at the end of a lesson. Children should be encouraged to use their journals at other times too.

IN CONCLUSION

To conclude, we have reproduced on the next two pages Daniel's and Jonathan's responses to *Alexander, Who Used to Be Rich Last Sunday*. Their work demonstrates the very special quality of shared book activity. Here the children used the familiar story pattern as the basis for their improvisations. They used the mathematics that they felt confident with, tailoring the activity to their own level of expertise, and each brought his personal experience and interest to the activity. Daniel's story was a straightforward improvisation on the original, personalised by his own device for signalling each time he lost some of his earnings. Jonathan added a new dimension by introducing a time line that was essential to his story. He showed that he was operating successfully with large numbers and with the passage of time, two features that another type of activity might not have allowed him to demonstrate. Shared learning experiences are ideal for mixed ability and multi-aged classes.

Daniel, Who Used to be Rich Last Saturday

Last Saturday I Used to be rich. I had earned
$25.00 with doing my jobs. Last Saturday
when I used To be Rich we went to the
Ekka I looked at a game stall and at the back
of the stall was a big Panda that I just
had to have that big Panda. The stall
was a clown game $2.00 a go and the score
to get it was 30. There were six numbers
1 to 6 and you got 5 chances You need 5 6's to
get the Panda. I went over to the stall to have
a go I got one, two, four, three, five, I did not
have anaf to get the Panda so I had a
another go but this was wost all ones's
by by $4.00. I was really saving the rest of
my money. To make shore of that we went
to the cattle to have a look. I saw this cow
for $10.00 I bought it mum told me not to
because it was really a bull I found that
out when it stared chasing me by by
$10.00 I was just realy realy saving
the rest of my money ontill we went to
the sample bag show. I bought the
Dirty things bag, Dirty trikes bag
and the Horrya bag then I had finished
all my money. As soon as I got
home I tried all my trickes on mum. Mum
therw them in the bin by by $11.00
Next year I'll try to save up all the
money I get.

Jonathan, Who Used To BE R ICH Last Year

Knock Knock knock who's there, the man from the pools.
Well don't just stand there come in, click clack. Well speak up
man just don't stand there. You have just won $700,000. 700 dollars
is that all. no 700,000 dollars. Wooo Wow wa exel ent, ha nd it
over. I can't, you have to go down to the pools to get your money. The next
day I went down to the pools to get my money but they couldn't find it so
I said if it's not at my place at precisely 12.30. I'm going to ring the police.
When I got home it was 11.00 while I was waiting I had a walk down the
he street and half way down the road I found a $20 dollar note. When I
got home I put the $20 dollar note in my wallet and looked at the clock it
was 11.30. In 15 minutes I put the kettle on and made a cup of tea.
In half an hour it was 12:15, I said to myself in fiffteen mins I'll
have $700.000 in fiff teen minutes I'll have $700.000. Ten mins went pass
and I was getting nerves. Two minutes went by and I started to ring the
police half way through the number I heard Knock Knock Knock.
Here's your $700.000. oh thank you, thank you thank you. Would you like
a cup of tea or coffee I said no thanks. I'm going right down to
the car deallers right now to buy some cars In 3 mins I was down
there I saw two Rolls Royces one for $300,000 and one for
$400,020. And I went home feeling very smart but
without any money and that is how I came poor again

8

ASSESSMENT

Showing what they know   *Evaluating themselves*
Involving parents

As teachers, we are 'accountable'. We need to know how our pupils are progressing so that we can modify our teaching if necessary, so that we can communicate with children about their progress, and also so that we can have informed discussions with parents and others.

So how can we assess children's progress while mathematics is in process? Before addressing this question in detail, we present one of our early attempts at assessing what a group of five-year-olds having difficulty with school maths could do, rather than what they could not do. This will provide a reference point for subsequent discussion.

While working as a remedial/resource teacher, Ann was recently asked by the Year 1 teachers 'to have a look at' some children who did not seem to be coping with their maths. The teachers had already been quite explicit about what these children could not do.

What could I do? I really wanted to give the children a chance to show me what they could do, what they did know and feel comfortable with. How could the children be put in a situation where they could show me what they knew? I had been writing a book about a little girl who likes numbers. Angela found numbers everywhere in the environment, but the number she liked best was the one on Grandpa's birthday cake, which she ate. I read this story to the children and asked them if they had any favourite numbers. This generated comments such as,

'I like six because that's how old I am.'

'I like ten best because that's the biggest number I know.'

The comments revealed information about the children's general awareness of the purpose of numbers and how and where they are used, and also about their number concepts. Quite clearly, David had had no experience of numbers past ten, and certainly could not count beyond ten.

Following this discussion, I asked the children to draw a picture of their favourite number. This also proved very interesting. As I observed the children, valuable insights into their understandings and motivations were possible. Not only was this activity valuable diagnostically, it also revealed a lot about the power of peer group tutoring. The description that follows attempts to show the type of problem solving and sharing as well as the diagnostic information that this activity generated.

Tami began tentatively drawing dot patterns beside her chosen numbers (in the same way as she would in class). She looked around and saw David happily drawing apples and decided to change over to fruit too. David asked,

'How do you write ten?'

Tami confidently drew a ten on her page to show him. Feeling very satisfied, she went on to draw ten oranges, counting as she drew,

'One, two...three...,'

She drew one more unnumbered orange and then stopped and began to draw two suns. David burst out,

'That's not ten.'

Tami said nothing and added one more orange. She looked at her new group of oranges, felt pleased and went on with her suns.

During this time Christopher had written and correctly illustrated the numbers four and five. Then he asked,

'How do you write eleven?'

I promptly showed him and everyone else stopped to look. Christopher copied the eleven and drew four circles. Mischa joined in, saying,

'You need more than that!'

Christopher added a few more, and Mischa asked,

'Is that eleven now?'

Christopher replied,

'I think so.'

and together they began to count, and shouted in unison,

'Not enough!'

One more was added, the counting repeated, another one added. They counted again and were satisfied. Now feeling confident, Christopher asked,

'How do you write one hundred?'

I showed him. Everyone looked, and on most papers somewhere 100 was written. Christopher did not attempt to draw anything beside it but went on correctly and confidently to count out ten circles.

Simon began by writing a five on his page. He drew one big car. As he was drawing it the other children began to tell him that it was too big and asked how he was going to fit five on his paper. At first Simon was unperturbed. He turned his paper over eventually, wrote another five and began to draw snakes. He drew one beautifully, began another, less beautifully. His concentration wandered and he began to bother the other children. Impatiently, Christopher said,

'I thought you were doing five.'

Simon looked at his page, changed the five for a two and went off to play with the blocks.

Mischa wrote the number ten and seemed to be enjoying the — for him — fairly tedious process of writing more tens. This was followed by a similar group of fives. He seemed to need this chance to practise his number formation. Later conversation with his teacher revealed that he is only now beginning to insert real letters into his scribble writing too.

John got started very quietly. Not a very confident child, he began with numbers he knew he could manage. When he wrote his number four he only drew three oranges before going on to five. Beside his five he drew three oranges. He looked at the row with three in and one by one matched the oranges in each row with his finger. He counted his five row, counted his fingers to three, put up two more and said 'five'. He had seen the light and quickly added two more oranges. At this point he noticed a pattern in the way the numbers were growing and realised that row four spoiled it. It did not take a moment now for him to realise that he needed one more. Quiet John was now busy showing everyone his pattern. Not to be outdone, Tami looked and looked at her paper and said,

'I've got a pattern too. Two pears and two apples. That makes four.'

Everyone looked and everyone parrotted her phrase, confirming for themselves that this was so. The bell called a halt to this.

With no pressure to perform or please the teacher, the children had demonstrated a willingness to try things out, to take criticism from peers and to solve the problems that arose. They had also demonstrated a natural curiosity,

'How do you write one hundred?'

'I've got a pattern too.'

that can lead them to push themselves forward to new mathematical ideas.

Sharing these comments and descriptions of what happened convinced the teachers that these children did actually know a lot that they could build on. The teachers were pleased when, over subsequent days and in similar contexts, most of these children began to use numbers more confidently in the classroom, working in small groups and sharing what they were doing.

Simon remains a problem. As yet he sees no real purpose in any of the three Rs. The question to battle with now was how to make maths meaningful to Simon — but that's another story.

SHOWING WHAT THEY KNOW

We have used this example of assessment because it highlights the point that process maths enables children to show what they know and how confident they are in what they know. Just last week at playgroup, two four-year-olds were playing hide and seek. They discovered that counting to ten did not give enough time to hide. They talked about this and neither of them could count past ten. Very quickly Melinda found a solution to this problem,

'Let's count to ten and then to ten again.'

Quite a sophisticated solution, don't you think? If we were writing a report card for Melinda wouldn't it be more appropriate to write,

'Can work out a strategy for solving a simple counting problem.'

than

'Can't count to twenty yet.'

By noting that a child can invent strategies to cope with counting beyond ten we can provide more such contexts, knowing and trusting that eventually counting to twenty will be more closely approximated; and just as the child learnt to count to ten, so via experience and exposure in meaningful situations, the child will, when ready, learn to count to twenty.

The Cockcroft Report brought the Seven Year Difference to everyone's attention. Within any one classroom, even in an ability streamed school, there are great differences not only in what the children can do, but also in how they do maths. Knowing that a child was in the bottom percentile last year and is still in that percentile this year does not help the child's self-concept or the teacher in knowing what to do about it. On the other hand, keeping anecdotal records and examples of children's work, and conducting interviews with children can result in an understanding of how a child learns best, how the child is actually progressing and also when to offer new challenges, resources or assistance. For example, Jason's teacher began making regular observations to see if she could find a way of improving his approach to addition. Her informal notes over a two-week period focused on what he was actually doing as he worked out his answers,

5 April   Uses objects to show his operations. Objects scattered everywhere.

6 April   Touch counts objects to five accurately and then loses track of which he's touched.

11 April   Knew 5 + 5 so didn't work it out. But worked out 7 + 1. Set himself more additions and each time used objects to find answers.

13 April   Asked Jason what he does when he goes shopping. He uses his fingers to count on. Did his sums correctly by this method today.

Using this approach Jason's teacher began to ask questions about her own programme in relation to Jason, about what she might do to help him and eventually about how Jason would cope with addition in the real world. She is now questioning not only her approach to teaching mathematics but also how different children can build on what they do know. Her comment to us:

> 'It's interesting really. I knew I ought to observe children but I didn't know what to look for or what to do about it. I'm learning as I do it. I can see two or three children doing the same things so I can have a conference just with them. When I get the hang of it more I don't think it'll be too much trouble. I thought I'd spend hours writing up my notes and things but that's not necessary, is it?'

Her two key strategies for assessment were making observations and maintaining checklists for each child.

OBSERVATIONS

As you watch children, brief statements can be noted down and if necessary expanded after the lesson. As you observe you can record:

- skills being used;
- strategies being used;

- errors being made and those being self-corrected;
- mathematical language being used;
- attitude to a particular activity;
- purpose for which the concept/skill was used;
- confidence with which the skill/concept was used;
- form of communication used (e.g. report oral/written, algorithm, diagram, illustration, model).

CHECKLISTS

These are easy to make and keep up-to-date and if used sensitively can provide useful information. Checklists where skills are ticked as they are taught or covered do not give a true picture of how a child is progressing. If a child uses a skill in one situation on one particular day, this does not indicate that the child 'knows' that skill. Checklists are only useful if they provide spaces to record the use of a skill in more than one context and for more than one purpose over a period of time. The type of checklists that we have found useful are shown below.

	Level of Attainment				
Strategy	**No evidence**	**Met, but not used**	**Used shakily**	**Used**	**Used coherently**
Try a simpler case					
Be specific					
Be systematic					
Find a good representation					
Look for a pattern					

EVALUATING THEMSELVES

Children know best how they are coping with a task and yet we seldom involve them in self-assessment. Quite often they do not even know what we teachers value in mathematics. A page of ticks seems to be the ultimate goal. When children choose their own topics they are in the best position to judge how satisfactorily they have achieved their goals. When teachers set the topics they can involve students in knowing what is expected. Together the goals to be achieved or the skills to be used can be made explicit to the pupils. For example, if the problem you set is,

'Which four odd numbers total fourteen?'

you might together talk about the importance of selecting an efficient adding strategy, of being systematic, recording results, looking for patterns and presenting results. The children will then know what they will be sharing as a group or class afterwards. They will be expecting to discuss or have a conference about addition strategies, for example, and will be prepared to share, compare and evaluate the efficiency of the method they used. They will see this as a natural and effective part of the learning process from which they can benefit and not as a test which they might fail. This type of self evaluation will eventually become self-initiated. Even when working independently on a project, children will reflect on their work and refine or correct as a natural part of their own learning process.

CONFERENCES AND INTERVIEWS

As you talk with children, giving them responsibility to discuss issues which concern them, it is possible to record, either as notes or on a checklist, aspects that children feel confident or concerned about. Also as children talk they will indicate their understandings and show clearly where they are starting from. Such information should be recorded for reference when you are planning either skills sessions or future activities. By involving children in these discussions you can, together, plan the next activities in such a way that ownership remains with the children, recording any decisions that you make.

INVOLVING PARENTS

If what we really want to know is how effective our teaching programme is, how the children are progressing, and how can we talk to parents about the class, we need more than a score on a test to help us. Saying to a parent,

'Oh, Billy scored 11 out of 20 on his test.'

is really not the basis for a discussion, especially if Billy was sick that day or mum and dad had had a row and his score is normally 19/20.

By continually observing children as they work in normal relaxed class-room settings, we gain an overall picture of a child, not just of how well he did on one particular day on one particular test. We are able to talk intelligently and positively to parents about what we have observed and to use anecdotes to support our statements. So rather than say to parents,

'Oh, Billy is about average at maths.'

you could look at your anecdotal records and say,

'Yes, Billy has a thorough understanding of measurement. Last week when we were doing some informal measurement he invent-ed a very interesting method of finding how far it was downstairs. The class was delighted and soon tried his method. Billy used a calculator to find his answers because the numbers were too large for him to work with...'

This then invites a dialogue with the parents about what Billy is doing at school and how he is doing it, and also offers scope for the parents to support this work at home.

DATED EXAMPLES OF WORK

Alongside these anecdotal records, dated examples of children's work can confirm or refute any assumptions that you make about a child's progress. By referring to several dated examples of a child's work you, the children or parents can discuss the progress being made. Careful analysis of several pieces of work can show changes in a number of ways. For example there might be changes in:

- the range of the numbers that the children choose to work with;
- the strategies being used;
- the presentation and layout of the work (this can indicate changes in attitude and confidence);
- development in the thinking processes being used (being system-atic, trying a simpler case, representing etc.).

The use of methods such as keeping observations, maintaining check-lists and filing dated examples of work will result in a profile of each child that shows clearly what they can do and where they are starting from. This profile can then become the basis from which you and the children can work together to plan and negotiate future development in such a way that the children will have responsibility for their own learning and can retain ownership of their work. Confidence will de-velop from this type of feedback, where the children can see how well they are doing, rather than feel how poorly they might be doing.

IN CONCLUSION

With traditional mathematics testing, the children sit down and answer twenty or so pencil and paper test items. Usually these test items atomise skills to such an extent that they in no way reflect or allow children to use the strategies that they may have developed to cope with maths in the real world. A typical example here is the difference between the subtraction algorithm taught in schools and the counting-on method usually used in real life. Traditional testing emphasises the answer and end product, rather than the processes used to achieve that answer. Little, if any, diagnostic information can be gleaned from this type of testing.

More valuable information about the processes and strategies that children can use is gained by observing children as they work individually or in groups on activities in context. As children work they will reveal information about how they find answers, their use or otherwise of concrete objects, their ability to select appropriate resources or units, the elegance and efficiency of their methods and their use of related language. As you observe, there is scope to talk with them about how they are proceeding and why and, most importantly for you, there are opportunities to give feedback which children desperately need. This feedback can take the form of confirmation, supports or on-the-job help. Children learn best when the need arises, not after the event.

PART THREE

INTO THE CLASSROOM

- ◆ Introduction
- ◆ Devising a Curriculum
- ◆ The Classroom Environment
- ◆ Activities to Try

INTRODUCTION

It is our belief that mathematics is a developmental learning task in the same way that learning to talk, ride a bike or swim are developmental learning tasks. In this kind of learning, you don't learn little bits and pieces and store them away until it's time to put them all together. Rather you start from the whole and learn the little bits as you go along. Two analogies from our own experiences are swimming and bike riding.

At school we learnt to swim on dry land during the winter. We stretched out over a bench and learnt the arm movements. Each week we came a little closer to getting them right. Then, when we had mastered the arms, we learnt the leg movements. Then came the really difficult part of putting the two together. Later still, we had to learn to breathe. When summer came and we went swimming in the water, we went swimming all right — right to the bottom. We'd learned a lot about swimming strokes, but not about swimming. We did learn, though, in the water by practising and doing it.

Bike riding is difficult, of course, without a bike. To ride a bike, you get on and try it. You fall off, graze your knees, but all the time you know you're going to master it. Not a bit at a time, like balancing, then steering, but all in concert. Learning to ride a bike has other features of developmental learning too, like, for instance, really wanting and needing to ride a bike to visit friends, go to school, be like your peers, have fun; like doing it in your own time and taking responsibility for how far and how long you'll practise at any one time; like the immediate feedback (you know when you get it right or wrong).

Mathematics learning could have these qualities too, if we would let it — if we focused on purposes for using mathematics and provided conditions in the classroom that make learning mathematics a natural developmental process. And that's the focus of Part Three.

In Chapter 9 we look at how to design a curriculum that makes a mathematics in process approach possible. In Chapter 10, we explore ways in which the conditions for learning can guide us in creating a suitable classroom atmosphere. Finally Chapter 11 suggests a number of activities for you to trial in your own classroom.

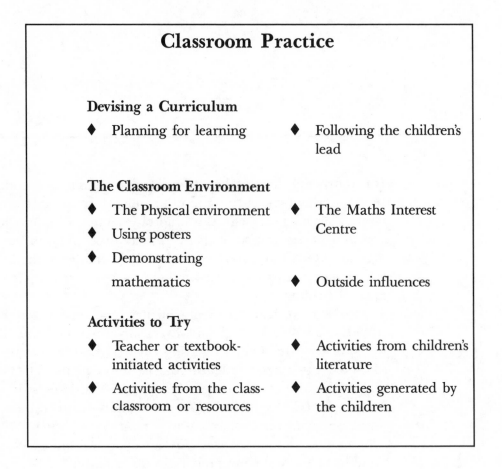

Classroom Practice

Devising a Curriculum

♦ Planning for learning

♦ Following the children's lead

The Classroom Environment

♦ The Physical environment

♦ Using posters

♦ Demonstrating mathematics

♦ The Maths Interest Centre

♦ Outside influences

Activities to Try

♦ Teacher or textbook-initiated activities

♦ Activities from the class-classroom or resources

♦ Activities from children's literature

♦ Activities generated by the children

9

DEVISING A

CURRICULUM

Planning for learning   Following the children's lead

Following through the earlier descriptions of mathematics in process, the question we want to address is how to devise a curriculum that reflects the process view. If we look at the implications of Parts One and Two of this book, we find that curriculum design should have certain features that characterise it:

1. **Ownership generates the will to learn**. A range of mathematical topics is required, from those imposed by the teacher to those generated by the children. But the most effective way of encouraging learning is to allow children space for ownership of their own mathematics.
2. **Learn mathematics by doing mathematics.** Here the implication is that the skills of maths — mental arithmetic, measuring, multiplication, etc. — will be acquired best when the need for learning is generated by involvement in a mathematical activity.
3. **Mathematics is for communicating.** The feedback obtained from an audience's reactions to mathematical communication is invaluable in supporting learning and in the development of skills.

We first need to ask how we can effect a change of ownership. Currently, all impetus for activity comes from the textbook or teacher. Can we not find ways of involving the children in framing their own questions and topics for investigation? The implication of the assertion 'Learn mathematics by doing mathematics' is that we need to rethink much of what passes for maths teaching in our classrooms. The emphasis needs to shift from teaching to providing opportunities for children to mathematise in the sure knowledge that this will lead to learning.

PLANNING FOR LEARNING

As well as informing us about the nature of mathematical activity, its process and purposes, the frameworks suggested in Parts One and Two also provide tools to help in planning how a particular mathematical topic could be presented in the classroom. The four-part framework of Part One:

- experience of problems;
- mathematical activity;
- communicating results;
- reflecting

suggests a flow for the individual events that we should plan for, while the eight purposes,

- describing
- explaining
- planning
- designing
- choosing
- transacting
- predicting
- investigating

can be used to suggest contexts in which the events might take place. To show how this works out in practice, we have taken the topic 'Sharing' as our example and pitched it at the eight-year-old level.

INITIAL IDEAS

When devising an outline for a topic, we find it best to begin with a brainstorming session. The first stage is a very rough draft, sometimes produced as a list, other times as a topic web (see example opposite).

An alternative is to review the activities described in maths schemes or state guidelines that are relevant to the topic in question. Often only minor adaptations are needed for these activities to match a particular purpose.

When planning your introduction to a topic, it is always sensible to start where the children are, which means asking whether there is a process with which the children are already familiar that could lead them to think in terms of the topic in question.

MAKING A PLAN

At this stage the outlined ideas need to be fleshed out. This can be through discussion with colleagues, or by writing more extended notes. The key to this stage is using the process headings of Part One. For instance, with 'sharing', we planned an activity that invites the children to sort a set of everyday objects into equal-sized groups. We then used the process framework of Part One to flesh out this activity.

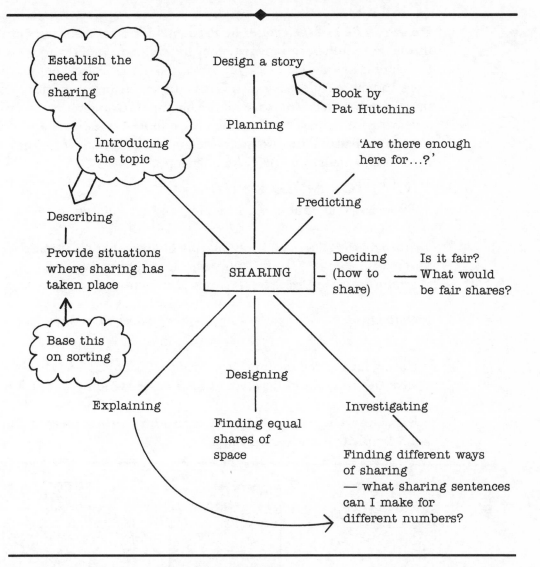

Establish the need for sharing

Introducing the topic

Design a story

Book by Pat Hutchins

Planning

'Are there enough here for...?'

Predicting

Describing

Provide situations where sharing has taken place

SHARING

Deciding (how to share)

Is it fair? What would be fair shares?

Base this on sorting

Explaining

Designing

Investigating

Finding equal shares of space

Finding different ways of sharing — what sharing sentences can I make for different numbers?

EQUAL-SIZED GROUPS

Experience of problem	Identifying criteria for sharing
Mathematical activity	Exploring different ways of sharing
	Recording results of sharing
Communicating results	Demonstrating and describing methods and results to another group
Reflecting	Recording in journal

Central to this activity is asking the children to *describe* their groupings and to comment on anything particular that they noticed.

This kind of sorting activity asks the children to find their own reasons for the grouping within the context of the objects provided. The alternative would be to suggest the reasons and challenge the children to find suitable objects (both in kind and quantity). As an example, the story *The Doorbell Rang* by Pat Hutchins takes a simple sharing theme that could be improvised on by the children. In the story a group of two children have a plate of twelve cookies to share, the doorbell rings and more children appear. This happens again, and again, until there is only one cookie per child, whereupon Grandma arrives with a new trayful. An activity in which the children investigate and write about a similar situation would provide many opportunities for the children to experience the need for sharing.

THE DOORBELL RANG

Experience of problem   Listening and responding to the story

Mathematical activity   Exploring similar sharing situations
Improvising on the story

Communicating results   Reading stories to rest of class
Making class books

Reflecting   Commenting on stories and range of sharing in each

Having introduced the topic, we then looked for activities that would involve the children in developing their understanding of sharing in different contexts.

For example, there could be some spatial work, where areas of shapes could be divided into equal parts,

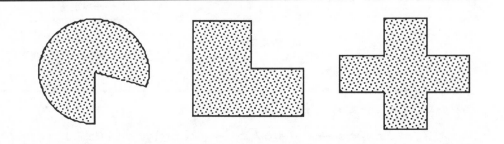

and the children could also be asked to *design* their own shapes for sharing.

SHARING SHAPES

Experience of problem   Discussing which shapes will be easy to share, which will be difficult

Mathematical activity   Folding, cutting, comparing parts
Discussing which pieces have same area but different shape

Communicating results   Comparing results with other groups
Making 'Sharing Shape' posters

Reflecting	Any surprises?
	Extending to other shapes

We also included an activity which asks the children to *investigate* different ways of sharing objects, with the choice of number of objects being left to them. This might well lead to their finding that some quantities (e.g. twelve) are 'good' for sharing while others (e.g. thirteen) cannot be shared equally in any other way than one each. Here it would be important that the children choose their own objects and quantities as this not only allows them to bring their own thinking to the investigation but also encourages them to operate at the level at which they themselves feel comfortable. The children could be asked to *explain* their findings to the rest of the class.

GOOD NUMBERS FOR SHARING?

Experience of problem	Discussing what is a good number for sharing
Mathematical activity	Investigating ways of sharing different numbers
	Recording results for each number
Communicating results	Sharing and comparing results
	Collating findings on a class chart
Reflecting	Drawing conclusions (introducing the terms composite and prime)

The idea of 'fair shares' could also be used, and the children could *choose*, for example, what would be fair to charge for an outing, how to share out a bottle of drink etc. Perhaps the success of this activity would depend on the extent to which we encourage the children to *transact* as they reach their conclusions.

FAIR SHARES

Experience of problem	Brainstorming what would be involved in going on an outing
Mathematical activity	Working out costs
	Deciding on 'fair shares'
Communicating results	Presenting information
	Reporting decisions
Reflecting	Would it work?

A third way of developing the children's understanding of 'sharing' would be by means of a calculator activity. Initially the challenge could be,

'How many eights in ninety-six? Estimate and check.'

Here we would be inviting the children to *predict* the outcome of sharing and then use calculators to check the outcome of their predictions.

SHARING ON THE CALCULATOR

Experience of problem   Making initial rough estimates
Mathematical activity   Using strategies for estimation
Calculating
Choosing new numbers
Communicating results   Comparing strategies for estimation
Comparing different keystroke
sequences (e.g. using repeated
addition)
Reflecting   Discussing how estimation helps
with sharing problems.

We might conclude these activities by inviting the children to *plan* a display of their results.

Woven into many of these activities would be opportunities for the children to explain what they have found out. This could be done 'on the job' by having some of the activities being undertaken in groups, or as a whole class. Alternatively, the children might write their own explanations of sharing in their personal journals. This might lead to the children generating their own ideas for investigation, and such opportunities would be encouraged.

At various stages of all these activities, the children would be asked to reflect on what they have learned and anything they have problems with. Some children might like to construct their own 'What I Know about Sharing' lists,

'I know how to share fifteen among five — three each, and among three — five each.'

'I can't share 17 — there's always some left over.'

Reflecting could also encourage the children to consider the methods of sharing that they have used,

'Give everyone five then see what's left over.'

'For equal shares give one to each person, then do it again until you run out.'

This would emphasise the possibility of different strategies for 'sharing' and would focus on the 'how you know it' aspect of reflecting rather than the product of sharing which is the 'what you know' aspect.

CHECKING THE PLAN

Before putting the learning plan into action, we find it helpful to construct an overview, one that shows how each activity covers the purposes framework. The chart at the top of the next page shows this for the 'sharing' topic.

Topic: Sharing

	Experience of problem	Mathematical activity	Communicating results	Reflecting
Planning	A Sharing Story — *The Doorbell Rang*			
Designing		Dividing shapes up into areas		
Investigating	Different ways of sharing a given number of objects			
Describing	Grouping objects by different characteristics			
Explaining			Reporting findings and personal dictionary	
Predicting	Calculator-based estimation of sharing			
Transacting			Class shop/post office	
Deciding			Journal write-up and demon lists	

This kind of chart clearly shows any gaps or areas of overkill that have been created by the plan. For example, the chart looks rather light on *explaining* and *transacting*. Perhaps we should modify our ideas, or at least ensure that we make time for these aspects to take place. This could be achieved if we were to ensure that the activities included natural breaks where groups working together could explain their findings to the rest of the class. Perhaps each item in the class display on the topic of 'sharing' could be introduced by its makers who could explain what it shows.

FOLLOWING THE CHILDREN'S LEAD

Ownership within activities such as those suggested above will be achieved by children as they develop and refine situations imposed by the teacher, but open for them to pursue in their own ways. This process of ownership should, of course, be encouraged within the possibilities/parameters offered by prepared activities. Occasionally, however, children will bring their own ideas to the front and will need to be supported to follow their own avenues. Here is an example from Ann's own classroom scrapbook.

JONAH AND THE WHALE

I had been teaching for two years when I first 'heard' my class's plea to be allowed to follow a course of activity that interested them. We had been reading 'Jonah and the Whale' as part of religious instruction. I of course milked it dry, directing attention to the 'moral' of the story. Lesson over, I instructed the children to get their journals out, but there was so little response and so many long faces that I had to ask them what was wrong.

The questions began,

'Are whales really that big?'

'What's the biggest whale ever found?'

'Could a whale really swallow a man whole?'

So much for my plans for the day. The *Guinness Book of Records* had to be fetched from the library and the facts read out. And now another barrage of questions,

'About how long is 31 metres?'

'Is it as long as our playing field?'

'How high would it be?'

There was no stopping them now. They had to answer their questions and as they answered one question, another six seemed to stem from the answer. Pretty soon they were asking questions like,

'How many children standing side-by-side would be as long as a whale?'

'How high would it be in the middle?'

Quite complicated maths was under way. Out into the playground again went the class, lining up side-by-side and instructing me to measure the line. Back in school the children wanted to know how many children there were on roll, were there enough to stretch out the full distance of the whale? Long division and multiplication was integral now to a solution to this question. Towards the end of the day sub-groups have formed, to carry out some kind of investigation or research, and were busy writing reports about the size of whales. Now the demand was for a real audience, in this case the whole school, to report to. The head teacher was very impressed, so too was the rest of the school, but it was not the children who reaped the reward. No, it was all accredited to me, for surely I had instigated, and organised the whole affair. I just wish it were true... I'd love to be that talented.

That was the first time that I let children react and respond in a free way to input, direct or indirect. The story had aroused cognitive dissonance in the children — they had to find answers to their own questions. It was an important day for them, the day they realised that they could generate questions, find information and do mathematics to answer those questions.

So what was special about the day Jonah took over our classroom? First, I guess, was the fact that we had during almost a year together created a genuine sharing, trusting environment in our room. The children had obviously accepted this atmosphere and were beginning to assert themselves as questioners and thinkers, and for the first time wanted to create contexts of their own.

Secondly, as the questions were theirs, they needed answers, they were in the driver's seat. Given this responsibility the children generated a range of complex questions, questions much harder than I would have predicted they could possibly answer. They developed investigations and strategies of great sophistication and practicality to find their answers.

Lastly, they sustained this work, even through lunchtime, to find their answers and later to structure their reports. They knew when a satisfactory (to them) conclusion was reached and they had total ownership and felt confident that others would be interested too.

Of course Jonah does not come along every day, so what can we do to help children who want to explore mathematics? As stated elsewhere, children have learned much about mathematical thinking before they come to school. They have, for instance, had many experiences first or second hand of filling/emptying containers, estimating when to stop pouring, constructing, watching buildings in progress at the construction site, seeing older siblings or parents fitting pieces together to make something, seeing the shopping process, setting the table, counting. They have seen it on television, in counting books or positional books like *Rosie's Walk*. In fact they are what Cambourne describes as 'immersed' in mathematical thinking within their everyday lives. This need not stop when they pass through the school gates. Like Claire and her bedroom design dilemma, encourage the children to bring their problems and ideas in through the gate with them.

10

THE CLASSROOM ENVIRONMENT

The physical environment   *The Maths Interest Centre*
Using posters   *Outside influences*   *Demonstrating mathematics*

Before children come to school they are what can only be described as 'vital'. That is, they are full of life, curious, questioning, ready to engage in and sustain activities. School takes this vitality and lets it wilt, not deliberately of course, but by cutting off the life supply, the freedom to think, enquire, explore and sustain activity. In short, by providing what are often closed, uninspired activities that require little thinking about and are meant only to last for twenty minutes or so.

Of course, this is not what we as teachers intend. We honestly try to engage children's interest and motivate them. What we haven't done is to try to give the children any say in the choice of activities or to get to know our children well enough to be able to 'start where the children are'. Nor do we tune in readily to the noises children make when something interests them.

Let's look back to the conditions for learning that Cambourne proposes,

- immersion
- demonstration
- expectation
- responsibility
- approximation
- employment
- feedback

and see how we can use them to help us create an appropriate classroom environment. For example, how can we immerse children in whole, meaningful and purposeful mathematical contexts where they are provided with opportunities and inspiration to have mathematical ideas? Below we list some techniques and ideas that have worked for us and for the children we have worked with.

THE PHYSICAL ENVIRONMENT

Immersion is dependent on the physical environment of the classroom. Neither blank walls, nor walls covered in everything but maths, is likely to foster the view that maths is valued or an interesting topic. The walls can be used to display, for example, environmental print, children's own mathematical work, professional mathematical posters, photographs of work in progress, children's own algorithms or strategies illustrated for others to try. For best effect, make sure that each new display is looked at and discussed. Encourage the children to take time to observe independently and try out things displayed. Above all, do not leave the displays up too long; it is the initial impact that children respond to. In one classroom some children had made a collage of a postman putting a letter into mailbox 38. No sooner was this on the wall than children were asking,

'What does that number say?'

'What's it for?'

'What's my house number?'

Within the next day or two these five-year-olds had made a number strip around the room and written their names on the corresponding house numbers. The next stage was the desire to write and address letters to each other. Pockets were made and fixed to the number line so that letters could be delivered to the actual address. Again, it was the children who generated the questions and the purpose for this work. They organised it, asking for support in demonstrating the writing of the numbers but actually writing them themselves. They wanted to deliver letters so invented pockets. They learnt their own house number as well as those of many friends. In short, they had ownership and responsibility for their own extended mathematical project, changing and refining it as they needed to.

In another classroom we observed a group of children spontaneously trying to follow a child's wall poster with instructions for making a net for a number seven. Painstakingly these children tried to make their sevens. It didn't work. There was the expected noisy frustration until one of the group asked,

'Why doesn't it work?'

Now the children in the group were folding the nets and looking at the defects of the model. Almost as one, they began trying to make their own nets that would work. They struggled with different arrangements and began writing their instructions for a '7'.

'What other numbers can we make nets for?'

was the next question.

Situations like these enable children to take *responsibility* for their own learning. They decide what course an activity will take and how far to pursue it, and they know when they are satisfied with the results.

THE MATHS INTEREST CENTRE

Maths Interest Centres are another means of fostering conditions for mathematical learning. A Maths Interest Centre works best when it is set up as a comfortable, non-threatening part of the room where the children can, in their own time, come to explore the resources, examples of children's work, or problems displayed there, or just quietly explore a maths topic of their own. Within the security of such a setting, the children can take risks, trying out ideas and refining them, i.e. making their own *approximation* to formal mathematics. A good rule for a Maths Interest Centre is to change the displayed resources frequently. For example, over a period of a week, everyone who wants to, can find a few minutes to spend there. During the second week some children will be disappointed that there is nothing new.

How do you set up a Maths Interest Centre? One way is simply to display a new resource. For example, set out several pairs of compasses and scrap paper. Over the next few days children will come to explore the potential of a pair of compasses, will struggle with how to use them and will make designs using them. The children can then display their work in the Maths Interest Centre, if they want to, writing and illustrating simple instructions for using compasses to create designs. This, in turn, will stimulate more activity. At the end of the week a class book can be made of the children's work, and left in the Maths Interest Centre for future reference and reflection, or be taken home by children wanting to continue this activity. In this way, the children will feel able to take *responsibility* for what they do. It should be their centre as much as yours, even though you would have charge of the resources displayed, which will reflect the age and interest of your class.

An alternative to setting out pairs of compasses, for example, would be to set out a random collection of objects, such as string, tacks, chalk, pencils, rulers, paper, scissors, tin lids, and a challenge card — 'Invent a gadget for drawing circles'. Children's instructions for making their gadgets could be displayed in the centre for others to copy, try out or be inspired by.

One teacher we know displays 'two problems for the week' in her Maths Interest Centre, along with a wide range of resources that could be used to solve them. Her children display their results, and record their strategies for solution, in the centre. The children love to compare their results and methods and frequently try out other children's methods.

In short, stimulus for the Maths Interest Centre can come from class work, resources, problems, and challenges.

USING POSTERS

When children's work is presented as a poster, it provides an audience and purpose for the work. By carefully phrasing and illustrating a piece of work for a poster, children are in effect employing the skills they have just learnt. *Employment* is a key to seeing how we can use maths and the power it has to communicate about and help understand the world in which we live. Reading other people's posters demonstrates this employment aspect. Just as in language we talk or write to communicate, so too in mathematics we can use our mathematical findings to communicate.

If we look at the range of posters in our environment, we see that their key functions are to inform, persuade, and compare. Class-made posters can have these functions too. For example, after work on exploring tessellating shapes, a comparison poster can be made:

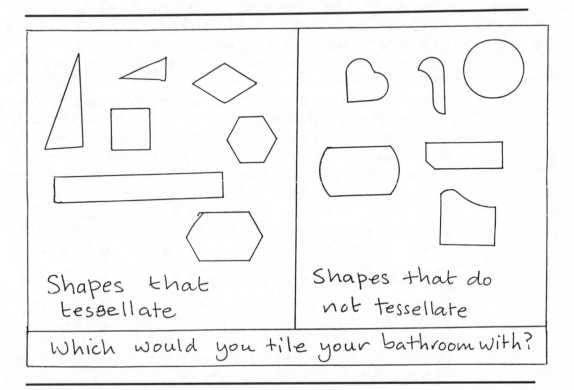

Shapes that tessellate

Shapes that do not tessellate

Which would you tile your bathroom with?

An arithmetic session on finding different ways of making a chosen number could result in a poster designed to inform:

Did you Know that
$6 \times 3 = \boxed{18}$ and so does 3×6
$2 \times 9 = \boxed{18}$ and so does 9×2
$1 \times 18 = \boxed{18}$ and so does 18×1

Did you notice anything special about these examples?

The use of bold print to pose further questions for the looker to ponder makes posters eye-catching and functional. They could also have space provided, like a graffiti board, for other children to add ideas or questions. Used in this way, posters can become a classroom resource rather than simply decoration.

Posters can also be used to illustrate the strategies that children use when solving certain types of problems. Strategy posters can be a class effort where all children contribute, and the teacher records. Children can then take responsibility for one aspect of the poster, writing explanations and examples more fully, and adding any illustrations needed to clarify them. Strategy charts such as these can be used to summarise strategies and are most helpful at the reflection stage as they encourage children to step aside from the problem, and provide a focus for discussion. If the children become stuck in problem solving, a strategy chart can also be used to encourage them to consider what they have been doing and whether there is another approach that they could try.

OUTSIDE INFLUENCES

Other stimuli for mathematical activity have arisen from objects brought into school, events in and outside of school, free exploration of maths equipment, and many others. In one classroom two children were trying to persuade the teacher that they should be allowed to move because their part of the room was the hottest, and it was so hot that it was making them 'dreamy', as the teacher called it. The teacher responded by saying,

'Well, prove it and you can choose where to sit.'

This demonstrated the teacher's *expectation* that the children would find a way of collecting information that might prove their point. It didn't take long for these 9-year-olds to hunt out a thermometer, but it took them a little longer and some patience to master (themselves) how to read it, and to cope with the frustrations when they realised that they wouldn't get an immediate response. When they did get results to present to the teacher they were told that she was not convinced that just because that was the hottest spot in the room now, it would necessarily be the hottest spot all day. They did not win the case, but they gained satisfaction and confidence as a result of their work.

There are many other examples of mathematical activity developing as responses to a variety of stimuli. What we must remember though is that we cannot force children to try out ideas or even try to persuade them to answer questions that we generate. What we can do is to provide *feedback* that:

- encourages them to generate such questions or ideas themselves;
- allows them to have ownership of their ideas and work;
- encourages them to react and respond to wall displays;
- encourages them to pursue their investigations for extended periods of time;
- supports them as they 'draft' and 'redraft' their thinking, their models, representations, symbolisations, reports and investigations until they are satisfied with their results.

DEMONSTRATING MATHEMATICS

Although not all teachers enjoy maths, all teachers can share in the discovery process. Occasionally join in with the children. *Demonstrate* to them that you sometimes grapple with a problem, pursue a wrong alley, get frustrated, try again. Let them see your thinking strategies as you work systematically towards a solution. Share this with your class so that you grow together. When you have some personal calculations to do, demonstrate your involvement with mathematics to your class, either saying,

'You get on with your maths, I've got some of my own to do.'

or by drawing them into your activity, for example,

'I'm going to buy curtains after school today. I measured the windows. There are four at 132 centimetres and one at 65 centimetres. I need to allow 10 centimetres for hems and I need two curtains at each window...'

The children could help you step-by-step to your answer or choose to work on it on their own. Either way, they will see how maths is used in everyday life; they will see a person they respect using maths to find important answers and they will see maths being integrated — number, space and measurement — to solve a problem.

IN CONCLUSION

Providing a physical and emotional environment where this type of activity can happen requires not only careful arrangement of the classroom fittings but also, and more importantly, a set of explicit classroom rules and expectations. Children need to know when they are free to talk and move around the room and when they are expected to be quiet and still. They need to know the difference between a working buzz and distracting noise. Perhaps your room could have a quiet corner where children who want to be left in peace can go and work.

Children will also need guidance in how to hold discussions and offer suggestions, criticisms and praise in a sensitive way. You will be, unconsciously, a role model. Children soon pick up and copy their teacher's intonations, ways and expectations and attitudes.

11

ACTIVITIES TO TRY

Teacher or textbook-initiated activities
Activities from children's literature
Activities from the classroom or resources
Activities generated by the children

At a recent conference we decided to help the audience appreciate how simple it can be to offer children an open-ended activity. Hoping that the audience wouldn't notice that we were experimenting with them, we took two problems and posed them in both an open and a closed manner. Half were posed:

Problem Sheet 1

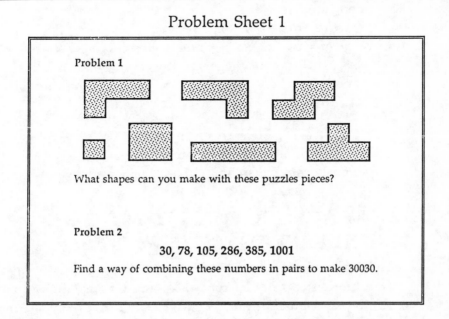

Problem 1

What shapes can you make with these puzzles pieces?

Problem 2

30, 78, 105, 286, 385, 1001

Find a way of combining these numbers in pairs to make 30030.

while the other half worked on:

Problem Sheet 2

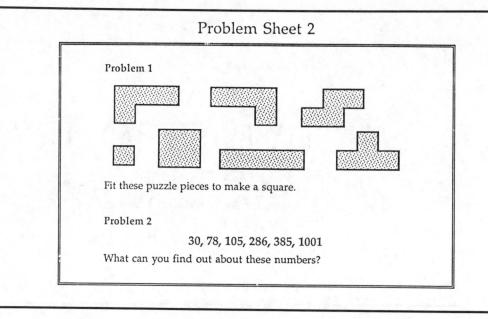

Problem 1

Fit these puzzle pieces to make a square.

Problem 2

30, 78, 105, 286, 385, 1001

What can you find out about these numbers?

For nearly ten minutes we left the audience to work in groups. And work they did, but one half spent the majority of the time working on the open problem, which, in its closed form, the other half had completed very quickly. In a feedback session we found that the open or 'goal-free' statement had in each case led to a wide range of outcomes and approaches. In this case, the audience were all practising teachers, but children too react in similar ways to open-ended opportunities.

In this chapter we explore ways of ensuring that you have a wide range of 'goal-free', open-ended activities to get started. We also offer ideas to help you begin generating your own ideas and activities. We've grouped these ideas into four categories that indicate the main sources for activities. These are activities which,

- are teacher or textbook initiated
- come from children's literature
- arise from classroom activities or resources
- are generated by the children.

TEACHER OR TEXTBOOK-INITIATED ACTIVITIES

We begin with this category for two reasons, the first being that it makes a gentle step from current classroom practice into a mathematics in process approach. The second reason is that there will be times when you want to introduce a new topic. This could be a topic that you don't think the children will initiate themselves or a topic from your mathematics syllabus that you need to ensure has been covered adequately.

TRAFFIC SURVEY

Teachers have many favourite activities that they know children will enjoy and engage with, for example,

> 'We are going to go out to the school gate and tally the traffic that passes the school so that we can make a graph.'

Children do seem to enjoy this type of activity but they never 'own' it. They've been told what to do and why and how to record their findings. Most of the purpose and need to think mathematically has been taken away from them. That's no reason to abandon this topic though, as with a little thought the activity can become something that children care about and want to work on.

There are two things that can be considered here. The first is the possibility that, if you wait, you will hear the children complain,

> 'The crossing guard makes us wait till all the traffic goes by, even when there's a big space. It made me late for school.'

> 'My mum has to drop me right round the corner because this street's got so busy.'

in which case the children may want to investigate just how busy the road is. The other thing to consider is how to rephrase the original statement so that it leaves scope for the children to assume some responsibility for the shape that the activity takes, for example,

> 'It's a nice day so I thought we'd go out and do a traffic survey. I'd like you to decide what you'll survey and why. In groups talk about how you'll record your information and what you'll do with the results.'

The children can now generate their own questions and make them match their own interests or curiosity. Children in this type of context generate questions like,

> 'My dad's got a Toyota, he says there are more Toyotas on the road than any other car because they're the best. We're going to see if it's true.'

> 'We're going to see how many cars go by in a minute and if it varies much during the day.'

> 'Sometimes we can't hear bits of the story when we read out loud because of the trucks that go past. We're going to see which vehicles are noisiest and how many of each there are.'

Questions like these may not lead to a much wider and more challenging range of mathematics being used than the original statement would have. But the children in answering their own questions will become involved in the topic and therefore motivated.

The children will also be involved in making the decisions as to what and how to record. In this context, they may want to construct a database of their survey findings, which they can add to over a period of time. A database of this kind will enable them to explore, for example, whether there are long-term trends in the information they collect, whether the proportion of cars to trucks changes on particular days, which makes of car are most common etc. Finally, they will have a reason to communicate and something to communicate about to the rest of the class or a broader audience.

Let's see how this description can be developed into a lesson plan:

TRAFFIC SURVEY

Experience of problem
Whole class (allow 10 minutes)

Could arise from the children's experiences or could be teacher posed, e.g.

'We are going to do a traffic survey. What information should we collect and why?'

Mathematical activity
Groups (allow 20 minutes)

Brainstorm and list children's ideas. Children decide what information to collect and how to record their findings.
Have a trial run.

Communicating results
Whole class (allow 5 minutes)

Discuss and compare appropriateness and efficiency of methods used.

Mathematical activity
Groups (allow this to take up to 25 minutes. This would complete the first lesson)

Refine plans and methods.
Carry out survey.

Survey as often as is needed to collect required data

Record and collate information after each survey. Encourage the children to devise and refine their own methods of recording (this could be on a database).

Communicating results
Groups and whole class (allow 40 minutes)

Prepare a report/poster on findings. Report findings to rest of class.

Reflecting
Whole class (allow 20 minutes)

Reflect on what was found out, methods used for data collection and recording.
Comment on how informative/persuasive the reports are.
Discuss what general principles of survey design can be gathered from this experience.

ODD AND EVEN NUMBERS

Many topics that you know you need to deal with can be introduced in this way. Odd and even numbers, primes and composites for instance can be explored and discovered by the children themselves if you ask,

'Using between one and thirty counters what different rectangles can you make? Keep a record of your findings for later.'

A topic like this will be approached differently by each group and may well lead to a discussion about whether a one by something row can count as a rectangle. Some children will discover that only even numbers make a two by something rectangle. Others may discover the prime numbers. At report back time further investigation will be initiated by the general discussion. This is also a time for you to introduce any appropriate terms. Class books or displays will provide reflection and revision of the topic.

Compare this with a more traditional introduction to odd and even numbers,

'Which numbers can you share equally between two people? Which numbers can't you share equally between two people?'

which tells the children what to discover. We wouldn't expect this activity to last for longer than one lesson, although the resulting class Big Book or display should be available for reference for a week or more.

ODD AND EVEN NUMBERS

Prepare collections of 30 counters, enough for the children to work in groups of three or four.

Experience of problem
Whole class (allow 10 minutes)

Ask the children to explore what different rectangles they can make.
Allow an initial hands-on period during which the children experiment.

Communicating results
Whole class (allow 10 minutes)

Discuss and compare initial findings.
Highlight methods and encourage systematic approaches.
Discuss methods of recording.
If necessary, ask whether all numbers make a rectangle with two rows.

Mathematical activity
Groups (allow 20 minutes)

Continue and complete exploration.
Record and collate information during exploration.
Encourage the children to look for patterns/draw conclusions.

Communicating results
Whole class (allow 10 minutes)

Report findings to rest of class.
Introduce the terms odd/even (and prime/composite if appropriate).

Reflecting
Individuals (allow 10 minutes)

Write about/illustrate findings for class Big Book.
Discuss 'What I know now that I didn't know before'.

TAKING SHAPE

Another technique that works well (introduced in Chapter 1) is that of not clearly defining a problem, or of only partially posing a problem, for example,

> 'Using four red, six blue, eight green and twelve brown Unifix cubes what can you make or find out?'

gives the children little indication of what's expected. You can almost hear the children say,

> 'What does she want us to do?'

After an initial discussion, each group will find something interesting to do, make or investigate. Responses will be diverse, for example,

- growing shapes and predicting the next number needed in the series;

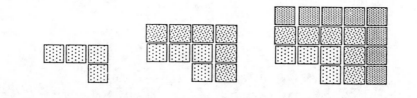

- deciding whether it matters that ten Unifix were not included in the original list;
- making patterns with the objects,

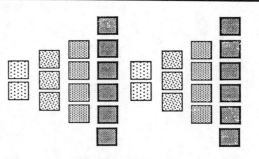

- describing the groupings,

> 'They're all in the two times table.'

> 'They're doubles, four and eight, six and twelve.'

> 'The next in the series would be sixteen and twenty-four.'

The sharing of each group's findings would then generate more questions and avenues to explore. The value of partially defined problems is that the children decide what the question is and in so doing take ownership of it as well as tailoring it to suit their level of ability. But times needs to be set aside for the children to decide how they will define the problem, and, if some children find it difficult to make this decision, our lesson plan should allow time for them to pick up ideas from others. Here is how we would plan a lesson for a 'Taking Shape' activity.

TAKING SHAPE
Prepare sets of Unifix cubes for each group.

Experience of problem *Groups (allow 10 minutes)*	Pose the problem: 'Using four red, six blue, eight green and twelve brown Unifix cubes what can you make or find out?' Encourage the children to explore their own ideas about what they think the problem is and what they plan to do.
Mathematical activity *Groups (allow 10 minutes)*	Encourage the children to follow up their plans and to make a start on their investigations.
Communicating results *Whole class (allow 5 minutes)*	Discuss and compare each group's line of investigation, the methods used and preliminary results.
Mathematical activity *Groups (allow 25 minutes)*	Continue the explorations or investigate ideas offered by other groups. Encourage the children to record their findings for a class book.
Communicating results *Whole class (allow 10 minutes)*	Talk about what has been discovered and the different methods of recording used.
Reflecting *Allow time during the next week for the children to read the resulting Big Book*	Collect reports and sequence to make a class Big Book.

CALCULATOR QUICKIES

Textbook activities can be treated in the same way, for example,

'Enter a two-digit number on your calculator. Give the calculator to your friend. Can your friend make one addition to total 100?'

This calculator quickie sets a task for the children to do but at no point do they have any real involvement in the activity. They are only required to follow the instructions given. With very little change however, this could become an extended piece of work that caters for individual differences within the class. For example, invite the children to,

'Make up your own rules for a calculator quickie and change the starting numbers if you want to.'

Here, the type of operation and range of numbers used can ensure that every child can work at his or her own level. The children choose a number and a rule and work out and perhaps record the answer before inviting a friend to play. Our lesson plan for this activity would be:

CALCULATOR QUICKIES

Provide one calculator for each pair of children.

Experience of problem
Whole class grouped in pairs
(allow 5 minutes)

Pose the problem:
'Enter a two-digit number on your calculator. Give the calculator to your friend. Can your friend make one addition to total 100?'
The children try out this activity and suggest ways in which they could vary the problem.

Mathematical activity
Pairs (allow 30 minutes)

The children make and test their own Calculator Quickies, deciding:
• the rules/operations to use
• the range of numbers
• what strategies to test
The new games are recorded.

Communicating results
Whole class (allow 15 minutes)

The new games are tried out on others.

Reflecting
Whole class (allow 10 minutes)

Did the games encourage the use of strategies for calculating?
Did we need the calculator?

TIME FOR...

Very closed activities like the time activity that follows can be made more purposeful by providing a context.

What time is it?

The children could, for example,

- write stories using the times shown;
- suggest situations where knowing the time is vital (e.g. planning a robbery or manoeuvre, clocking in on a rally, giving out medicine in hospital, choosing a television show, catching a train) and use these times as the time line for a story, rearranging them to suit their story line;
- make up a riddle about each time so that others can guess which time they are thinking of, for example,

'If it was this time in the morning I'd be asleep. If it was this time in the afternoon I'd be getting ready to go home from school. What time is it?'

Stories and riddles like these can be made into displays or books for others to read and use. This will provide a sense of ownership and motivation to tell the time. The most popular resource in the classroom is often the one produced by the children. Here is our lesson plan for this activity.

TIME FOR ...

Provide pictures of clocks showing different times.

Experience of problem
Whole class (allow 10 minutes)

Talk about the times showing on the clocks, e.g., 'What do we do at each of those times?'

Mathematical activity
Groups (allow 20 minutes)

The children order the times to make a story sequence, or make up riddles about the times.

Communicating results
Whole class (allow 5 minutes)

Share stories/riddles with the rest of the class and comment on the results.

Mathematical activity
Groups (allow 15 minutes)

Prepare final drafts of stories/riddles for a class book.

Communicating results

The class book can be put in the Maths Interest Centre, or sent to another class for their enjoyment.

Reflecting
Whole class (allow 10 minutes)

Have fun setting a clock and making up strange time tales, for example, 'It is 4 p.m., which is a strange time for breakfast, unless you are a koala.'

In these examples, we have focused on how teacher or textbook-initiated activities can be modified in a way that opens the doors to mathematics in process. To conclude this section, we revisit some of the activities mentioned in Parts One and Two of this book and suggest ways in which such activities might develop in the classroom.

ACTIVITIES FROM CHILDREN'S LITERATURE

We have found that children's literature provides opportunities for children to experience and experiment with mathematical language (and hence concepts) in ways that bring their own personalities to the fore. There are many excellent books for children that have a mathematical theme, and in most instances children will respond to these books with very little prompting.

STORY BOOKS

Story books provide settings, themes and characters that children can identify with and that stir their imagination and curiosity. Sometimes, as in *The Wonderful Pigs of Jillian Jiggs*, the children want to check the mathematical implications of the story. For example, after reading the story, children begin to ask,

'How many pigs did Jillian make?'

which is not a straightforward counting task in this book. They also ask,

'How much could Jillian have earned?'

'Ten cents is a bit cheap, isn't it?'

These are questions that the children really want to work on themselves, and the outcomes of their activity are surprisingly inventive and expressive. When drawing up a lesson plan around a book like this, it is important to build in opportunities for the children to respond in their own way to the story, even when the story suggests questions to you that you feel the children should attend to. You can always come back to these questions if necessary, i.e. if the children find it difficult to respond to the story in their own way. Here is our plan for using *The Wonderful Pigs of Jillian Jiggs* as the basis for a lesson.

THE WONDERFUL PIGS OF JILLIAN JIGGS

Experience of problem
Whole class (allow 10 minutes)

Read the story to the children, pausing for them to comment or predict. Encourage them to talk and generate questions about the story.

Mathematical activity
Whole class (allow 5 minutes)

The children use the illustrations and information in the text to answer their questions.

Experience of problem
Whole class (allow 15 minutes)

Focus on the instructions for making pigs, and challenge the children to design their own creature (using classroom resources).

Mathematical activity
Individuals (allow 15 minutes)

The children design and construct their creatures, writing instructions as they go along.

Communicating results

Instructions to be made available in the Maths Interest Centre for others to try.

Reflecting
Whole class (allow 15 minutes)

The children use their own creatures in a retelling of the story.

PROBLEM POSERS

One Bear at Bedtime, Clocks and more Clocks, The Hilton Hen House, How Many Ropes on a Boat? and *Changes, Changes* are examples of books that pose mathematical problems. By pausing as you read, the children can be encouraged to predict possible solutions to the problems. 'The Case of the Growling Dog' in *Encyclopedia Brown Shows the Way* poses a detective problem that requires estimation of measurement in its solution and leads to the setting up of a scientific and mathematical investigation to find out if it's actually true that a footprint made in wet mud shrinks as it dries.

Although *Changes, Changes* is a picture book without words, it nevertheless has appeal to all ages. For example, we have seen 11-year-olds ask questions about this book that have led them to quite sophisticated investigations and recording. These children were fascinated by the fact that each construction was made from the one collection of bricks. They began to ask questions about balance and building design, and this led them to make their own collections of solid shapes and explore what could be made with the pieces. They then decided to illustrate their own versions of *Changes, Changes* which required them to master the drawing of three-dimensional shapes. The resulting books and sets of shapes were shown to, and used with the children in the pre-school. The children's response to this book was something of a surprise to us, and we didn't have a plan of what would happen. However, in hindsight, we would replicate this lesson with a lesson plan such as the following.

CHANGES, CHANGES

Provide materials for making shapes.

Experience of problem
Whole class (allow 10 minutes)

Invite the children to tell the story as you show the pictures.
Encourage them to talk and generate questions about the story.
The children use the illustrations to answer their questions.

Mathematical activity
Whole class (allow 45 minutes)

The children make their own 3D shapes in card or polydrons and use these to construct their own buildings/vehicles/ animals, whatever they prefer.
The children make up their own stories based on their constructions, and illustrate them.

Communicating results
(at a time that suits both classes)

The stories are shared with the children of another class.

Reflecting
Whole class (allow 5 minutes)

Discuss problems encountered in making and illustrating the shapes.

FACTUAL BOOKS

Factual books too generate mathematical curiosity and investigation. For example *What Did You Eat Today?* leads quite naturally to children asking and exploring questions like,

'What do I eat in a day?'

'What do our pets eat in a day?'

'Whose pet eats most?'

'What's most? More items or more weight?'

A group of children reading *Postcards from the Planets* decided to make a time line for the journey so that they could get a better feel for the distances between planets. They then researched how far apart the planets are with a view to working out how fast the space shuttle was travelling. *The How and Which Book* was used as a model by one class who decided to make up a similar question and answer book. They used their own class as the reference point, with trick questions like,

'Who has the longest hair?',
Jane, turn to square 21,
Priscilla, turn to square 25,
Frances, turn to square 30.

Frances had short curly hair, but when stretched her hair was surprisingly the longest.

THE HOW AND WHICH BOOK

Experience of problem
(Individuals, over a period of time)

Leave a copy of this book in the Maths Interest Centre to allow the children to explore the questions in it, and to become familiar with the format.
Challenge the children to make their own 'How and Which' book.

Mathematical activity
Groups (allow 15 minutes)

The children make up their own questions, based on information they collect from their own research or facts from books.

Communicating results
Groups (allow 10 minutes)

Encourage the children to test out some, if not all, of their questions on another group.

Mathematical activity
Groups (allow 35 minutes)

The children consolidate their questions and work out a method of placing the questions and feedback frames in the book.
Make the books.

Communicating results

The new books can join *The How and Which Book* in the Maths Interest Centre for others to enjoy.

Reflecting
(at a suitable time)

Hold a readers' feedback session on the books that were written.

The examples given here all show how children respond to literature. You can of course suggest activities after reading a book, but we would urge you to allow time for the children to respond in their own way before you introduce your activity. We would also urge you not to ruin a good book by forcing the maths out of it or by overworking a book. If the mathematical theme is strong, this won't be necessary and if the mathematical theme is weak this won't work anyway.

ACTIVITIES FROM THE CLASSROOM OR RESOURCES

In the real world mathematics is rarely used in isolation from a context or purpose. Number is usually used as part of an activity such as working out how many Christmas cards or screws or paper napkins are needed, or in measuring activities.

In the classroom too, much mathematical activity can arise from a variety of topics, topics that span the whole curriculum. We need to become sensitive to these opportunities because in such instances the three strands of mathematics (number, space and measurement) are integrated, just as they usually are in the real world. Also in these situations the children are spontaneously employing a variety of purposes for using mathematics. Typical examples include,

- letting the children handle tuckshop orders and money (transacting).
- organising and making classroom books and displays (designing).
- collecting, recording and reporting on a science activity, such as plant growth (describing and explaining).
- sharing the workload on a class project (choosing).

The making of class books is becoming an established feature of classroom activity, and in itself is one that can call for a mathematical approach. There are decisions to be made (and researched) when publishing a book, decisions about book size, number of pages, layout and sequencing, all with a particular audience in mind. We could plan for this activity as follows:

DESIGN OF A CLASS BOOK

Experience of problem *(Allow 10 minutes)*	A collection of material needs to be published — have a brainstorming session to identify what factors need to be considered.
Mathematical activity *Groups (allow 20 minutes)*	The children generate the specific questions that their group will investigate and collect some initial data.
Communicating results *Groups (allow 10 minutes)*	The groups report on their questions and collect feedback on the information collected.
Mathematical activity *Groups (allow 20 minutes)*	The children consolidate their recommendations, collecting extra information as required.
Communicating results *Groups (allow 5 minutes)*	The recommendations are put together for a preferred book design.
Reflecting *(At a suitable time)*	When, at a later stage, a book has been made to the preferred design, have a brief session discussing the finished product.

Classroom resources too can provide a wide range of mathematical activities. Quite often we introduce resources to the children and tell them how to use them. From then on the children generally always use the resources in that way and for that same purpose. Base ten blocks are a case in point. They are often formally introduced as the material to use in place value. How to use them is modelled or explained to the children. Further exploration is cut off. From then on the box of base ten blocks is just that boring stuff you use to help you do sums, and no wonder teachers wean kids from them as soon as possible. Imagine a context instead in which the children are encouraged initially to play freely with the blocks. What might they discover? Here is what children in one class discovered when playing with base ten blocks for the first time,

'One base ten block is a centimetre. We measured our desk with them, except we used the strips. There's ten little ones in a strip. Then we just used six little ones to finish off!'

'We built with ours. We discovered that it was hard to stack up more than seven or eight so we used the strips. We made a cube like the big one out of ten strips. It took a hundred strips. We made everyone mad because we kept taking their strips. We're adding tens to see how many squares make the block. We've got four hundred so far! We think, we know it's more than eight hundred because we're not half way, we think a thousand.'

'We wanted to make a castle with towers, but we only had three cubes. We tried to stand four of the flat ones up to make the second tower. They wouldn't fit. The cubes have ten rows of squares. When you use flat ones it makes eleven rows. In the end we took ten flat ones and piled them up. That worked!'

These were just some of the responses, but from then we can see that even objects like base ten blocks can generate a great deal of mathematical enquiry. Here the children decided themselves that they needed names to describe the pieces. They all explored place value ideas quite spontaneously as part of their activity. After sharing what they did with the rest of the class the children are often observed trying out each other's ideas, like using base ten blocks for measuring and constructing.

USING BASE TEN BLOCKS

Provide base ten blocks for each group.

Experience of problem
Whole class (allow 10 minutes)

Allow time for the children to freely explore the possibilities of base ten books.

Communicating results
Whole class (allow 5 minutes)

The children demonstrate and explain what they have discovered.

Mathematical activity
Groups (allow 15 minutes)

The children try out ideas presented by others.

Communicating results

Labelled models or reports can be displayed.

Reflecting
Whole class (allow 10 minutes)

Discuss what has been discovered and when base ten blocks can be a useful resource.

ACTIVITIES GENERATED BY THE CHILDREN

Children, if we listen to them, often have things that they want to explore or follow through. In *From Puzzles to Projects* we talked at length about children posing problems that are important to them, problems like,

'What's a fair amount for pocket money?'

Children have other things that they'd like to investigate too, questions about their world, questions that they could explore themselves. For example, one day after story time the conversation turned to dogs in response to the story. One of the children was talking excitedly about her new puppy. This sparked Amanda who asked,

'My dog's seven human years. My mum says human years are longer than dog years. I want to know how old my dog is in dog years.'

The teacher told Amanda that each human year counted as seven dog years. Amanda looked around for some counting material and found her own way of finding out just how old her dog was.

Although she had had no formal introduction to multiplication or arrays, we see here how she quite naturally and spontaneously set out groups of seven counters, formed an array and then began to count. She had something that she wanted to mathematise about, something that she really cared about.

As teachers we need to listen to children as they talk and think out loud because very often they are verbalising questions that they really want answers to. This driving need and curiosity is the motivation to want to do some mathematics.

Children also have things that they want to do or make. We saw earlier in this book how a group of boys really wanted to make and fly a kite. Toy and model-making activities have great appeal to children and often require a great deal of integrated mathematics to complete. For example, during the craze for bouncing platforms, one bright spark thought the school balls could be adapted to make their own. Initially one trial ball was made after much experimentation. Issues to be dealt with were,

'How can we make a platform that's strong enough when all we have to work with is cardboard packaging?'

'What size does the platform need to be?'

'How can we make a circle that big?'

'What size circle do we need in the middle?'

At the end of this project the children had tested the strength of a variety of platforms, learnt a lot about circles, what radius and diameter were, how to construct a circle and so on. Although virtually impossible to plan for, activities that the children initiate can be expected to follow a course that we can plan, even though we are unsure of the starting point or the eventual conclusion. Steps such as those mapped out as follows are very likely to happen, and we can be prepared for them.

AN ACTIVITY GENERATED BY THE CHILDREN

Provide the necessary resources as they become needed.

Experience of problem
(Allow 10 minutes)

Allow time for the problem to be shared by the rest of the class, and for interest groups to form around particular aspects of the problem.

Mathematical activity
Groups (allow 15 minutes)

The children generate the specific questions that their group will investigate and collect some initial data.

Communicating results
Groups (allow 10 minutes)

The groups report on their questions and collect feedback on the information collected.

Mathematical activity
Groups (allow 20 minutes)

The children consolidate their work, collecting extra information as required and developing fuller conclusions.

Communicating results
Whole class (allow 5 minutes)

The parts of the problem can be assembled by the whole class to form a complete answer to the initial problem.

Reflecting
Whole class (allow 5 minutes)

Allow the last few minutes for the children to step aside from the work they have been involved in, and to evaluate what they have been doing.

Activities like these have real purpose for children who are therefore motivated to achieve. It is an important aim of the above plan to allow children to retain the initiative for what will happen. As they work on their problem, they will be using the mathematics they know and at the same time learning new skills that have immediate employment. They take responsibility for their project and the success of that project provides the only feedback they need. They also have the expectation throughout that they will find satisfactory solutions to their tasks.

IN CONCLUSION

Way back when, we, as teachers, thought all we had to do was to make space for problem solving and investigations in our maths programmes. In this book we have aimed to show that a problem-solving, investigative approach can become central to the way in which we teach mathematics. For the learner, mathematics itself is a problem to be solved, an investigation into the unknown, and it takes a problem-solving, investigative approach for mathematics to be learnt in ways that are both enjoyable and purposeful. This can come about when mathematics is in process in our classrooms.

CHILDREN'S BOOKS

Base, Graeme. *My Grandma Lived in Gooligulch*. Nelson, Melbourne, 1984.

Bond, Michael. *Paddington Hits the Jackpot*. Hodder & Stoughton, 1982.

Carle, Eric. *The Very Hungry Caterpillar*. Puffin, 1985. Melbourne, 1988.

————. *What Did You Eat Today?* Informazing series. Nelson, Melbourne, 1988.

Gag, Wanda. *Millions of Cats*. Puffin, 1982.

Gilman, Phoebe. *The Wonderful Pigs of Jillian Jiggs*. Scholastic, 1988.

Hinchcliffe, J. *The Hilton Hen House*. Ashton Scholastic, 1982.

The How and Which Book. Jacaranda-Wiley, Brisbane, 1986.

Hutchins, Pat. *Changes, Changes*. Bodley Head, 1975.

————. *The Doorbell Rang*. Puffin, 1988.

————. *Rosie's Walk*. Puffin, 1984.

Inkpen, Mick. *One Bear at Bedtime*. Collins, 1987.

Reade, Harry. *How Many Ropes on a Boat?* Reed, 1987.

Smyth, Gwenda & James, Ann. *A Pet for Mrs Arbuckle*. Penguin, Melbourne, 1981.

Sobol, Donald. *Encyclopedia Brown Shows the Way*. Penguin, 1980.

Viorst, Judith. *Alexander, Who Used to be Rich Last Sunday*. Angus & Robertson, Sydney, 1987.

SELECT BIBLIOGRAPHY

Baker, J. *Calculators in the Primary School*. Open University Press, Walter Hall, Milton Keynes, 1982 (also available from the Department of Mathematics, University of Queensland).

Baker, J. & Baker, A. *From Puzzles to Projects: Solving Problems all the Way*. Nelson, Melbourne, 1986.

Barnes, D., Britton, J. & Rosen, H. *Language, the Learner and the School*. Penguin, 1986.

Brown, S. I. & Walter, M. *The Art of Problem Posing*. Franklin Institute Press, 1983.

Cockcroft, W. H. *Mathematics Counts*. HMSO, London, 1982.

Collis, K. and Biggs, J. *SOLO: A Taxonomy of Learned Outcomes*. Arnold, 1976.

Dalton, J. *Adventures in Thinking*. Nelson, Melbourne, 1985.

De Bono, E. *Mechanisms of the Mind*. Jonathan Cape, 1969.

Graham, A. *Calculators in the Secondary School*. Open University Press, Walter Hall, Milton Keynes, 1984 (also available from the Department of Mathematics, University of Queensland).

Halliday, M. *Explorations in the Functions of Language*. Arnold, 1973.

Holdaway, D. *The Foundations of Literacy.* Ashton Scholastic, 1979.

Mason, J. H. with Burton, L. & Stacey, K. *Thinking Mathematically.* Addison-Wesley, 1982.

Parnes, S. J. *Creative Behavior Guidebook.* Charles Scribner's Sons, New York, 1967.

Parry, J. & Hornsby, D. *Write On: A Conference Approach to Writing.* Martin Educational, 1985.

Tough, J. *Listening to Children Talking: A Guide to the Appraisal of Children's Use of Language.* Ward Lock, 1976.

Turbill, J. *Now, We Want to Write.* PETA, 1983.

_____ (ed). *No Better Way to Teach Writing.* PETA, 1982.

Walshe, R. D. (ed.) *Donald Graves in Australia — 'Children want to write...'.* PETA, 1981.

Walshe, R. D. *Every Child Can Write!* PETA, 1981.

INDEX

Note: Activities are shown in **bold** type; children's literature is shown in *italics*.

questioning, 10–12, 20, 29, 38

Rapunzel, 103
reacting, 11, 41, 42, 56, 131, 137
recording, 53–6, 70, 106, 107, 116, 125, 135, 143, 145, 147, 149
redrafting, 2, 29, 42, 137
refining, 2, 4, 36, 52, 56, 104, 105, 130, 133, 142
reflecting, 2, 7, 9, 11, 45, 62, 63, 66–8, 70, 71, 78, 104, 107, 124, 125, 127, 128, 136, 143–5, 147, 149, 151, 153, 155, 157, 159, 161, 164
Report Writing, 71
reporting, 11, 41, 42, 56–8, 62, 69, 70, 104, 106, 127, 129, 131, 143–5, 159, 161, 164
representing, 77, 95, 99, 117
researching, 11, 26, 29–31, 104, 106, 156–8
responding, 58, 77, 95, 99, 131, 137, 146, 154, 158, 160
responsibility, 4, 76, 77, 88, 91, 92, 96, 107, 116, 117, 121, 131–4, 136, 141, 165
results, 2, 116
revising, 29
Road Safety, 58
Rosie's Walk, 131
rough draft, 124

sharing, 58, 69, 100, 124
Sharing on the Calculator, 128
solutions, 16, 25, 27, 30, 35, 52, 54, 56, 61, 100, 131, 135, 137
sorting, 13
specialising, 39, 40

The Spider and the Fly, 14, 68
spontaneous activity, 16, 19, 21, 24, 25
strategies, 4, 10, 42, 54, 56, 58, 60, 63, 69, 81, 104, 106, 113, 114, 116–118, 128, 131, 135–7, 149
summarising, 11, 26, 29, 30, 31
systematic *see* being systematic

Taking Shape, 146–7
teacher-posed activity, 18, 20, 23, 25, 122, 139
Theme Books, 104–6
Time for . . ., 150–1
topic web, 17, 19, 124
Traditional Rhymes, 27
Traffic Survey, 141–3
transacting, 77, 78, 83–5, 124, 129
Treasure Hunt Charts, 33
trial and error, 86
trying a simpler case, 117
Tuck Shop Orders, 53
20 Cents, 60

Using Base Ten Blocks, 161

The Very Hungry Caterpillar, 101
visualising, 33, 85

What Did You Eat Today?, 156
What is Special?, 18
The Wonderful Pigs of Jillian Jiggs, 152–3
writing, 10–11, 25, 41, 50, 52, 54–6, 78, 80, 95, 100, 101, 103, 112, 128, 130, 133–5, 153